D1559138

PREVIOUS BOOKS BY DAVE DILES

*Duffy*

*Nobody's Perfect*

*Twelfth Man in the Huddle*

# ARCHIE

# ARCHIE

## *The Archie Griffin Story*

## ARCHIE GRIFFIN
## WITH DAVE DILES

1977
Doubleday & Company, Inc.
Garden City, New York

PHOTO CREDITS

1—Courtesy of the Columbus, Ohio, *Dispatch*.
2, 3, 4, 5, 6, 27, 28, and 29—Courtesy of the Griffin family collection.
7, 8, 9, 9A, 13, 14, 15, 16, 17, 18, 19, 20, 21, 22, 23, 24, 25, and 26—
Courtesy of Chance Brockway.
10, 11, and 12—Courtesy of Barry Edmonds.
30 and 31—Courtesy of Arthur Corr.

ISBN: 0-385-12442-2
Library of Congress Catalog Card Number 76–51691
COPYRIGHT © 1977 BY ARCHIE GRIFFIN AND DAVID DILES
ALL RIGHTS RESERVED
PRINTED IN THE UNITED STATES OF AMERICA
FIRST EDITION

This book is dedicated to Fritz Howell, my mentor for many years while we labored together for the Associated Press. He could communicate, this man, simply because he understood and practiced the art of plain talk. He took a kid under his wing and taught him, and Fritz and Hylma made room for me in their home and in their hearts. Most of all, Fritz taught me that this thing we call sport—even at Ohio State—is not quite as important as The Second Coming.

Dave Diles

# ACKNOWLEDGMENTS

I'm grateful to the Griffin family, for being as nice as neighbors you would pick for yourself. I'm indebted to Marv Homan, the sports information director at Ohio State University, and to his assistant, Steve Snapp; to Coach Woody Hayes, for being himself, and to Paul Brown of the Cincinnati Bengals. I am particularly grateful to Evelyn, my lassie, for her generous work on the transcripts; to Lois Diles Bush, for recording every line written about Archie Griffin even though she has never understood the madness that is Ohio State football. For giving me the opportunity to write my first book, *Duffy*, and for believing in me enough to let me do Archie's story, but most of all for being a friend, there is a generous outpouring of gratitude for my editor, Larry Jordan.

Dave Diles

# CONTENTS

# 1

## The Enlistment and the Glory

It is twenty minutes until four in the afternoon, and the football game is over. But even after the official time has expired, there will be one more play, because North Carolina has scored on the final play of the game.

A few of the fans among the more than eighty thousand who have jammed into giant Ohio Stadium have begun inching toward the parking lots. But most have stayed, even though the temperature—in the midforties—is unseasonably cool for Ohio in late September.

They are on their feet, clapping their hands and cheering the Ohio State Buckeyes, even amid the anticlimactic activity at the north end of the stadium as North Carolina adds the point-after-touchdown. On the west sidelines the Ohio State players, clad in their familiar scarlet jerseys and gray pants, are involved in ritualistic back-slapping—all, that is, save one player.

He is on his knees, giving thanks. For Archie Griffin, saying prayers long had been more than just a bedtime ritual. It was his custom to pray several times during the day, and always before and after football games, for strength to do his best, for himself and the other combatants to avoid injury, and a prayer of thanksgiving after the battle was over. On this autumn afternoon, as was his custom, he was taking time to say thanks.

If the victory was particularly sweet for Archie Griffin, it was extraordinarily disappointing for the Tarheels.

They had been beaten, 29–14, because an unheralded freshman halfback set an Ohio State rushing record by running for 239 yards.

The crowd stayed on its feets screaming wildly as the coaches, Woody Hayes of Ohio State and Bill Dooley of the Tarheels, shook hands as their teams trotted toward the dressing quarters at either side of the south end of the stadium.

If Dooley, whose team had won nine games the previous season, was shocked, the fans were not. It was just the kind of start to which Ohio State fans have become accustomed: two games, two victories. The North Carolina coach could not have been any more surprised than Archie Griffin. Dooley was to say later, "I didn't even know they had a running back named Archie Griffin."

Archie didn't think the Ohio State coaches were that aware of it, either. After all, he was just a freshman. And in the season opener the previous week, he had been called on to handle the ball just once, late in the game, and things got jumbled up and he never even got his hands on the ball.

"I remember that play," said Archie. "Dave Purdy had gone in to quarterback and they sent me in when we were ahead, 21–0. He called an 18-sweep. The ball was pitched down about my knees, maybe a little bit lower. But I should have had it. I couldn't find the handle on it, and Dave recovered it. We lost five yards, and I came out right after that. It wasn't much, but if I had concentrated on the ball instead of the daylight I saw ahead of me, I could have handled it all right. It's a game I'd just as soon forget."

But football fans will always remember his next one.

As Ohio State prepared for the North Carolina contest, there was nothing to indicate that Archie was anything but a fourth- or fifth-stringer. When the game began, he was on the bench, and figuring that if the Buckeyes ran away with the thing he might get in for a play or two near the end.

Over the years, Ohio State teams have often performed poorly against nonconference opponents, and some Woody Hayes critics have hinted that the old master doesn't even let his teams work against nonconference plays, looking ahead instead to the next Big Ten foe.

In the early going against North Carolina, it appeared that this would be one of those long afternoons, like the ones in previous seasons against Colorado and Arizona and Texas Christian and Southern Methodist and these same North Carolinians. In their first two possessions, the Buckeyes had the ball for exactly six plays and had been victimized by a blocked punt and trailed 7–0 with only 5½ minutes elapsed. It was not a typical Ohio State ball-control afternoon. Tailback Morris Bradshaw had carried four times for twelve yards.

Assistant Coach Rudy Hubbard was working the phones in the press box. He was encouraging—some say screaming—for Woody to send Griffin into the fray. As Coach Hayes remembers it, Hubbard was on the sidelines:

"He kept telling me 'Griffin is ready,' and I just kept listening to him," Hayes recalls. "I just asked him, 'Are you sure?,' and Rudy kept telling me he was. He'd been telling me about Arch all week, and I kept saying, 'How can he be ready? He's only a freshman.' You see, I try to talk my coaches out of things, and if I can't, then I know they're really sure of themselves. I couldn't talk Rudy out of it, and we weren't getting the job done with our other tailback. We weren't moving the ball, so I finally called for Arch. Right away, as soon as he got his hands on the ball, you just knew that unless he got hurt, our tailback problems had been solved for the next four years."

Woody recalled that Archie's first carry was good for twenty yards. It was for six yards and so was his second carry and so was his third one before he was stopped at the line of scrimmage. But a man's memory can be hazy after nearly three hundred football games.

The second series after Archie entered the game, Ohio State drove from its own 22 to the North Carolina 5-yard line and got a field goal out of it. Archie gained 53 of those yards. He went outside his own left tackle on a 32-yard gainer that got the Bucks out of a hole.

The next time they got the ball, the Buckeyes drove 47 yards for a touchdown. Archie got 30 of those yards. There were two touchdown drives in the third period, and Griffin got 33 of an 87-yard march, then 70 yards on an 84-yard spurt. He went 55 yards down the sidelines on the drive that put Ohio State in front, 23–7. He got 30 more yards and his first collegiate touchdown in the final period.

He played only seventeen minutes, yet set an Ohio State single-game rushing record of 239 yards. He went on to total 793 yards during the regular season and added 95 more in the first of his four consecutive Rose Bowl appearances.

"What I remember most about the Carolina game is forgetting my helmet when someone yelled at me and told me to go into the game. I guess I was so shocked I couldn't think straight. I was already out on the field and the guys were screaming at me to come back and get my helmet."

And was it all that different from high school competition, when two-hundred-yard-plus games were commonplace?

"I didn't know what to think. I had some great blocking, and I kept seeing daylight so I just ran, that's all. There wasn't anything fancy about it. I didn't think it was easy. I didn't think much of anything, I suppose. I do remember coming back to the sidelines late in the game and I got down on my knees and, all by myself there, I knelt down. I just wanted to thank God for giving me some ability, and for the chance to play. It was all His doing, and I didn't want God to think that in all the excitement, I forgot about Him."

Archie remembers, too, that on the Monday after the North Carolina game, Coach Hayes strode up to him and said, "Arch, just remember, you may never have that kind of game again."

But it was the kind of performance Archie Griffin would repeat, time after time, the kind of performance that would three times earn him All-America honors and make him the only college player in history to twice win the coveted Heisman Trophy.

It was the beginning of a dream a young black from the East Side of Columbus would not permit himself to have just a few months earlier.

Before Archie Griffin got his diploma from Eastmoor High School in Columbus, Ohio, he knew he would trade his football skills for a college education.

Before he ever scored a touchdown in high school he was aware that his future plans included college. That's simply the way things are done in the Griffin household.

The thing that never occurred to Archie, nor anyone else, was how much he and the school he finally selected would benefit from his decision.

The recruiting of young men to play major college football may be, at best, a necessary evil. At worst, it sometimes can be a shade above a slave auction. It can boil down to little more than open bidding for beef on the hoof, talent by the pound. The measuring sometimes is done by speed per forty-yard dash, by strength in moving a huge blocking sled or the ability to catch a football in heavy traffic.

Archie Griffin originally wanted to attend Northwestern at Evanston, Illinois, and went so far as to write a letter to that school asking that someone come to watch him play football during his senior season at Eastmoor. Later he would ask his high school coach to call those in charge of recruiting at Northwestern. As it developed, that request would lead him away from Northwestern and to one of the giants of the gigantic business we call college football.

Archie might have opted for the Naval Academy, but the

thought of devoting four years to the military service after college turned him off.

He was impressed by Illinois because Bob Blackman, who was coaching the Illini at that time, actually came and talked with him.

He liked Don Nehlen, who was coaching at Bowling Green, and gave that school some thought. But had he chosen a school in the Mid-American Conference, it surely would have been Kent State. After all, one of his brothers had starred there.

Even though he was the standout prep player in Columbus—site of Ohio State University—Archie nonetheless visited the campus of the University of Michigan and liked what he saw. He had been strongly recruited by an assistant coach, Chuck Stobart, and once he got to Ann Arbor two of the Wolverines' stars, Billy Taylor and Gill Champman, had him in tow for a tour of the place and told him all the advantages of Michigan's rich athletic tradition. But it bothered Archie that the head coach, Bo Schembechler, was at home recuperating from a heart attack.

Like all high school standouts, Archie Griffin had his heroes, and one of them was Otis Armstrong, then a star at Purdue. Archie was impressed when he got to meet Armstrong on a visit to the Purdue campus.

He took an immediate fancy to the warmth and sincerity of Johnny Pont, then coaching at Indiana, and felt a little more at ease on the Bloomington campus since one of his buddies, Rodney Lawson, had gone with the Hoosiers the year before.

The recruiting had gone on, at a serious level, for more than a year. The letters from colleges and universities all across the country began arriving at the Griffin home, and at Eastmoor High School, after his junior season. Eastmoor had a good team, and Archie was the star—good enough to get third-team all-state honors. By the time he had finished a scintillating three-year career he had captured high school All-America honors, and more than a hundred scholarship offers awaited him.

There were no exotic trips to places like Florida and California, even though he might have taken them. First, it is not the nature of a Griffin, particularly Archie, to take advantage of anyone and to visit a campus he was not seriously considering. So he visited just a half-dozen schools. Besides, he was busy with his high school wrestling team once the football season was over, so he could never leave Columbus until late afternoon on Saturday.

"I had never been anyplace in my life," he said, "but I didn't see any point going someplace I knew I wasn't interested in. That'd be dishonest. All along, I had sort of made up my mind to go to a smaller school. Then I started thinking about Northwestern. I knew they never had a great record in the Big Ten, but I knew it was a good school, and I thought maybe I could play some there. That's when I wrote the letter."

Academically, Northwestern is tougher than most universities, but Archie's point average would have been good enough to get him in.

But why not Ohio State? After all, almost every strapping young man who grows up in Ohio dreams of putting on that scarlet-and-gray uniform, racing out into that huge horseshoe that is Ohio Stadium, hearing the stirring strains of "Fight the Team," and adding glory to the already lustrous heritage of Ohio State football.

Archie Griffin never allowed himself to have such dreams.

"When I was a little kid I used to hang around the stadium a little bit. We lived not far from there, and sometimes some of my buddies and I would walk down there on football Saturdays. We never got to go in. We never had tickets. We'd just hang around outside and someone would have a transistor radio and we'd listen to the game. A lot of kids did that. I guess I never thought much about going to school or playing football there, even when I was doing pretty well in high school. They really didn't recruit me very hard, and I guess I had lots of doubts about a lot of things, including my own ability. I wanted to play."

One of the long-time assistant coaches at Ohio State, Esco Sarkkinen, came to watch one of the Eastmoor High School work-

outs prior to the start of Archie Griffin's senior season. Archie had
a pulled hamstring muscle and didn't do much. He figured the
Buckeyes lost whatever interest they might have had. No one
from Ohio State mentioned anything about Archie going to
school in his hometown.

And when you stand only 5-feet-7 and weigh only 180 pounds,
you can put schools like Ohio State out of your mind with little
difficulty. You can do it easier if you're black.

Ohio State had aggressively recruited black talent, and some—
Brockington, Ferguson, and White—had become all-Americans.
But they were big, brutish running backs with the bullish power
that made Ohio's three-yards-and-a-cloud-of-dust offense famous.
But there was some "street talk" about Coach Woody Hayes. Not
much of it was the flattering kind. Lots of people in the black
community believed Woody had a violent temper, that he sometimes struck his players, and that he was prejudiced against blacks.
And that he was reluctant to play backs who were on the small
side.

No one feels lukewarm about Wayne Woodrow Hayes. To
many Ohio State fans, his greatness is second only to God's, and
some of the more rabid fans have trouble figuring out first and
second places. A handful, whose lives have another dimension and
whose emotional peaks and valleys don't depend on Ohio State
football fortunes, think Hayes is a maniacal martinet whose sin-
gle-mindedness brings him perilously close to madness.

It is a practice at Ohio State, as it is at hundreds of schools, to
invite promising high school players as guests to home games.
After the game the stars visit the locker room, and not infrequently the current Buckeye stars will hype the youngsters on the
virtues of Ohio State football. Almost without exception, Coach
Hayes stops by for a chat.

Archie Griffin's first visit to Ohio State came after a 20–14 loss
to Colorado in the second game of the 1971 season. Woody
Hayes had every reason to be upset. He's been known to accept
defeat with something less than graciousness, and his team had

passed the ball thirty-four times that day. There have been Hayes-coached Ohio State teams that have not passed that much in an entire season!

This was an Ohio State team that would lose three more times before the season ended; only once in a dozen years had the Buckeyes lost that many games. In only two seasons since Hayes took over in 1951 have Woody's teams lost more than they won.

"I thought maybe he'd ignore us from all I had heard," Archie recalled, "but he was nice as pie. We all introduced ourselves, and when I said, 'Archie Griffin of Eastmoor,' he shook my hand and said, 'You had a great night last night, son.' I had done pretty well. I scored 5 touchdowns and had something like 246 yards, and when he mentioned that, I'll have to admit it impressed me. It turned out he knew something about everybody in the room. I thought that was nice."

But Archie Griffin was not hooked then. And not after a second visit to an Ohio State home game and another tour of the Buckeyes' locker room. And not even after the Eastmoor and Ohio State seasons had been concluded and Coach Hayes invited him to a quiet dinner at a fashionable restaurant not far from campus. But Archie remembers every detail of the dinner, and the entire day.

"There was school, and afterward we had wrestling practice. I hurried home because I wanted to put on a coat and a tie. It wasn't a matter of trying to impress him, but I wanted to look my best. I think I was on time getting there, but Coach Hayes was already there. So just the two of us had dinner. He told me to order anything I wanted. I didn't even have to look at the menu. I knew I wanted steak. It was the first time in my life I had a regular steak—you know, a *real* steak—all to myself. I'd had cubed steak, but never a big porterhouse steak like I had that night. During my senior year Mom sometimes would cook one steak and my brother Raymond and I would split it, before a game. I don't think I was nervous that night. I know I had a good appetite. I ate every bite."

The two of them talked for an hour. The old coach did most of the talking but never once got around to football.

"He talked mainly about my education and how important it is for a person to get a good education. He started right off suggesting that I become a lawyer. You know, he's been pushing that ever since that night."

Perhaps the absence of football conversation indicated the coach had it in his mind that Archie Griffin, like most schoolboys in the state, would give his place in Heaven for a chance to play for Ohio State.

"I don't think so. I guess he thought I was interested or I wouldn't be there, and I guess I thought he was interested or he wouldn't be there. He didn't say much when we left the table, except that he enjoyed meeting me. He said we'd keep in touch, and that was it."

If Woody Hayes had known Archie Griffin then, as he would later, he would have understood that Archie would not give up his place in Heaven for anything else in the world. Archie was impressed, not awed. He was interested, not bug-eyed. His first choice still was Northwestern. If it could not be Northwestern, then it would be a smaller school.

All three of Archie's older brothers had gone to college, and all had excelled in football. Latty went to Louisville, Jim to Muskingum, and Daryle to Kent State. None would try to influence Archie. His father, James Griffin, Sr., would do it, though, but ever so subtly.

Much of the Ohio State recruiting had been done by Rudy Hubbard, later the head coach at Florida A&M. Rudy had played under Woody at Ohio State in the midsixties. Rudy was plagued by an assortment of injuries but bowed out in a blaze of glory, rushing for 103 yards and scoring twice in a victory against archrival Michigan in the final game of the 1967 season.

"I was real tight with Rudy. I think he was the first black assistant Ohio State ever had. He kept in close touch with me. What I liked best about him was that Rudy was up front about every-

thing. He stressed education, but he talked football, too. He did a
lot for my confidence, too. He told me I could play anywhere.
Lots of other schools put Woody down and said he didn't like
'pony backs,' but Rudy kept telling me I could play. He came to
our house a lot and spent time with our family. But there was no
pressure. He didn't lie about his feelings, and I didn't lie about
mine. He knew I was favoring Northwestern."

The patriarch of the Griffin family didn't lie about his feelings,
either. On the evening his fourth son was getting ready to visit
the Northwestern campus, James Griffin, Sr., said his piece briefly
and simply:

"Remember son, there's a lot of people around here who'd like
to be able to see you play football."

To young Archie, it was almost a mandate.

For the old man, it was practically a major policy address.

The older brothers said little, but Archie felt they may have
been leaning toward Ohio State. His high school coach, Bob
Stuart, never spelled out his preference and Archie never asked
him, but figured his coach leaned toward Ohio State. Friends had
their opinions, but all they did was add to the confusion. While
some openly campaigned for Ohio State, others whispered that
Archie could never make it there. They told him Coach Hayes
was a dictator, and a goofy one at that. They told him his size
would work against him and he'd get lost in the shuffle.

"I guess the psychology worked in reverse. The more I heard
that I couldn't make it, the more I was determined to do it. It
was a challenge to me, and I like challenges. I never liked being
told that I'm not good enough to do this or that.

"Finally I decided to talk it over with Daddy. I asked him right
out what I should do. All he told me was that it was my decision.
Larry was at Louisville and Daryle was at Kent State, and I had
signed tenders at both places. I knew my folks wanted to see all of
us play as much as possible, and that's why I signed those tenders.
Then I started thinking more and more about Ohio State. The
challenge of playing at a really big school against tough competi-

tion turned me on, and I knew if I made it, my folks could come and see me play.

"I wasn't given anything and I wasn't promised anything, not even that I would play right away. Coach Hubbard just told me he was sure I could play. My little brother Keith and I went out and had dinner again with Coach Hayes—I had another steak—and right there all of a sudden I just blurted out that I had decided to come to school at Ohio State. I don't why I did it right then. I just did it. Coach Hayes just said 'That's great,' and he reached out his hand and we shook hands and that was it.

"It was right between dinner and dessert, and I asked him not to say anything to the newspapers just yet, and he kept his word. I didn't visit another school after I gave him my word, and I didn't even tell my folks that night that I had reached a decision. But once I made up my mind, I never looked back, and I never have had any regrets."

The rumor factories are kept busy churning out stories about Ohio State's overzealous recruiting tactics. Books have been written about the Buckeyes' system of luring top high school talent to the Columbus campus. Woody not only swears up and down he doesn't cheat—even though one time Ohio State was slapped on the wrist by the National Collegiate Athletic Association because Woody gave some money from his television show to some of his players—and he admitted in 1976 that he blew the whistle on Michigan State for recruiting violations. There was a prolonged investigation by the NCAA and the Big Ten, and the Spartans wound up with a three-year probation and a ton of embarrassment. It did not heal the wounds any when Big Ten commissioner Wayne Duke announced, belatedly, that Woody Hayes was not the first coach to call "foul" against Michigan State.

It was Hayes who told his fellow coaches, "If I catch any of you cheating, I'll turn you in, too."

That's just one of the reasons that in some areas of the country you could assemble a serious lynching party more quickly than Woody's teams could complete a forward pass.

But Archie Griffin knows in his heart that his old coach would never cheat.

"With God as my witness, I never got a single thing that was illegal or immoral or anything else all the time I was at Ohio State. No one ever offered me anything, either. As a matter of fact, not one school that recruited me ever offered me anything under the table. I've heard all the stories, like everyone else, about cars and bank accounts and soft jobs and money in envelopes, but I never heard of one bad thing going on at Ohio State. That's the God's truth. People may think Woody cheats just because he wins all the time, but I don't believe in my heart he could cheat."

Archie Griffin lived in a dormitory his freshman and sophomore years and later had an apartment with some of his teammates. During the summer months he always went back home to live with his folks.

"I didn't have any fancy clothes, and when I finally got a car, my daddy bought it for me, and Coach Hayes was so upset when he saw me driving that car he made me go out and prove where I got it. Coach Hayes wins because he's a good recruiter, he gets good talent, and then he works hard. He works harder than any man I've ever known except my father."

Archie Griffin figured it was an even swap and a fair one: his football ability for a college education. Unlike many of the top stars at major colleges where football borders on a form of insanity, Archie got his degree and didn't dodge any courses. He was not in a five-year 'redshirt' program, either. As a matter of fact, he graduated one quarter ahead of time.

"It's just a little family game," he said. "The family has always competed, you know, making sure you make the team the first year, making sure you start, making sure you graduate. So I just wanted to graduate ahead of time, so I studied a little extra and got out in the spring instead of the summer of my senior year."

Before he did, Archie broke scads of records and won every award possible except best-dressed cheerleader. In a four-year career he became the first player in history to win two Heisman Trophy awards, given each year to the nation's outstanding collegiate player, and three times won All-America recognition. He became the darling of Ohio State fans, who long have been accustomed to football heroes. Archie was the greatest of the great.

Bob Ufer is a wildly colorful announcer who's done play-by-play for Michigan football for an eon, and he often has said that football at Michigan is not a sport, it's a religion, and Saturday is a holy day. His description could apply just as well at Ohio State.

Columbus is Ohio's capital city, and it sits smack-dab in the center of the state. Schoolchildren are told that if every one of the fifty states were cut off from each other, Ohio would survive longer than all the others, because of its versatility. It has not been ascertained whether that's a fact of life or a rumor accepted as such because of repetition.

The question is: Could Ohio survive without Ohio State football? The Buckeyes and their provocative coach surely are a total turnoff to some, but expressing contempt or even disinterest in the program is tantamount to treason and punishable by exclusion from barber shop conversations and coffee shop gatherings.

Coach Hayes' survival for more than a quarter century has been made possible by the enormity of his success and his own tenacity. Perhaps no man with such a low boiling point has such tough skin. He has more recognition than the governor of the state, more clout than the president of his university. It helps that he's had but two losing seasons in all his seasons there, and it helps that those who love him have a fierce loyalty that borders on idolatry. Detractors are akin to infidels.

When he lured Archie Griffin to Ohio State, Woody was not coming off a banner year. The Buckeyes had won six and lost four, and in years past at Ohio State that was cause for dismissal.

There were ninety-four players listed on the Ohio State varsity roster at the start of practice in 1972, Archie's freshman season. There were but two freshmen listed with the varsity, Archie and Brian Baschnagel. Even though he had just concluded an outstanding career at North Allegheny High School in the tough Pittsburgh area, Baschnagel did not rate a single line in the "Buckeye Personalities" section of the OSU football guide. Archie got nine lines that told about his having been named Ohio's high school back of the year and the fact that he had scored 170 points during his senior season at Eastmoor and that he had captained his high school football, track, and wrestling teams.

In the "Football Outlook" portion of the press guide, the publicity people pointed out that a "sporadic offense" had caused most of the Buckeyes' problems the previous season but that tailback Morris Bradshaw should give the Bucks a better wide attack and that "the key to success is held by the offense."

There was not a single mention of the fabulous freshman, Archie Griffin. Hardly anyone knew yet that he was fabulous. He endured the practice sessions as a fourth- or fifty-string tailback and spent much of his time working with the scouting team: For example, as Iowa was the first opponent in 1972, Archie spent the week working with fourth- and fifth-stringers, posing as Iowa players against the Ohio State varsity. Archie, and everyone else, figured him behind Morris Bradshaw, Elmer Lippert, Joe DeFillippo, and perhaps one other tailback.

After the record-smashing achievement in the second game of his freshman season, Archie Griffin would never be anything but a first-teamer.

Coach Hayes need not have cautioned Archie about the chances for a repeat of the North Carolina achievement. But if his star freshman needed a reminder about the peaks and valleys of athletic competition, he got it the following week against California: Archie gained only forty yards in fifteen carries.

"They were all over me. I knew it would be tough, but they showed me something that day. I remember getting hit a lot. They had made up their minds there wouldn't be any more of that two-hundred-yard stuff against them, and there wasn't."

Archie's longest gain in the victory over the Bears was for half a dozen yards.

He got 192 yards in his next game against Illinois.

"By that time, I was pretty confused. I wondered if I was getting into a habit of having one bad game, then a good one."

The Indiana Hoosiers were next, and Archie gained a modest sixty-five yards. "My old high school teammate, Rodney Lawson, was playing the monster back position for them, and we saw a lot of each other. He tackled me a lot, I remember that. He always was nice and helped me up, though."

The Buckeyes were 7–0 when they went up against Michigan State. The underdog Spartans upset Ohio State, 19–12 on the strength of four field goals by Dirk Krijt, a walk-on Dutchman playing in his first college game—and it was the first college game he'd ever seen.

"It was about the worst game I ever played," Archie said. "It seemed every time I touched the ball, I dropped it. I was just lousy, that's all."

Two fumbles, one of them recovered by the opposing team, were attributed to Archie, and he gained but forty-two yards in eleven carries. He paid for that performance the following week.

"We played Northwestern and we won the game, but my number was called only twice all day. I have to chuckle to myself when I look back on it, but it sure wasn't funny then. It was raining, and Coach Hayes decided to stick with the straight T formation all day long. I got my hands on the ball twice all day. I think I got eleven yards, then lost the ball on a fumble, in the third quarter. Then I got three yards later on. The rest of the day, the only time I saw the ball was when the referee took the towel off it and our center put his hands on it."

The Buckeyes prevailed, 27–14, with fullback Champ Henson carrying the ball a record of forty-four times and scoring four touchdowns.

There are many great rivalries in football, and to Ohio State and Michigan fans, theirs has more intensity than Yale-Harvard, Texas-Oklahoma, USC-UCLA or any of the other great ones. The indisputable fact is that there never has been a player on either side, playing in an Ohio State-Michigan game for the first time, who has been adequately prepared for the stress of the event.

"I couldn't believe it, and I'm not sure I can believe it after playing in four of those games. We got pretty excited about some high school rivalries, but this was like a war. I remember we had a meeting on the Monday before my first game against Michigan, and Rick Seifert wasn't gonna be able to play in the game. He was a senior and a real good defensive back, and he'd played against Michigan before. Man, he really gave us a talking-to. He tried to tell us about the importance of beating Michigan. He really got steamed up. I never heard anything like it in my life. It was like a preacher getting all caught up in a sermon.

"Now, I didn't let anyone see me, but I had big tears rolling down my cheeks. He got us all fired up. It was hatred—not real hatred, I guess, but it was almost like that, I guess. Then some guy who used to play for Ohio State a few years before came in, and he gave it to us some more. We had clippings all over the locker room. There was one that really got us going. The Michigan quarterback, Dennis Franklin, was from Ohio, and he said in this newspaper article, 'Only the really good Ohio players get to go to school in Michigan.'

"Once we got on the practice field, hardly anybody talked. No one talked all week. There was so much tension you really could feel it. Everybody was quiet, but when time came to play the game, we were prepared. It was the hardest hitting I ever experienced."

It was quickly apparent that the Wolverines were as fired up as the Buckeyes, and their main target was Archie Griffin. His first four carries resulted in zero yardage, and Michigan moved in front, 3–0, while Ohio State couldn't even get a first down in the first quarter.

The fourth time Ohio State got the ball, Michigan learned that it really was true: As Archie goes, so go the Buckeyes. He took an option pitch for ten around left end. Three plays later he squirmed free at right tackle and gained eighteen. In seven plays

Ohio State drove in for the go-ahead touchdown and never relinquished the lead. The 14–11 victory sent Archie and the Buckeyes hurtling to the first of four straight Rose Bowl games. Archie had set up the first touchdown and scored the second.

The Rose Bowl game was a nightmare. Archie fell on somebody's shoe on the first play and suffered a hip pointer.

"That's no excuse, though. I played. They were just a better team. They had Sam Cunningham, Anthony Davis, Charles Young, and a lot of other dandy players. I thought they were a pro team, they were so good."

It was 42–17 in favor of Southern California, and Archie accounted for ninety-five yards on the ground. It was a 9–2 season, much better than the previous season but not what Ohio State fans rate as excellent. But with Archie leading the way, things promised to get better. And they did, right off the bat.

In the 1973 season opener against Minnesota, the Buckeyes raced in front 14–0 before the season was seven minutes old. The opening drive was sixty-six yards long, and Archie got forty-two of them. The Gophers fumbled the ensuing kickoff, and Ohio pounced on the ball at the Minnesota twenty-three. The Bucks sent Archie off tackle for fifteen yards, and three plays later it was 14–0.

Then came something that was so typical of Griffin's career. Despite the Buckeyes' reputation as a fullback-oriented team, it was Archie they turned to in trouble, and it was Archie who put games out of reach. Minnesota roared back for a touchdown that narrowed the score to 14–7, but Archie grabbed the kickoff and went ninety-three yards for the score that broke open what might have been a close contest.

"I remember that, but I remember Neil Colzie ran one back, too, and Cornelius Greene had a super day. We won the game 56–7, and all of us figured we had a pretty good team."

The Buckeyes were more than pretty good. They routed Texas Christian 37–3, and Archie had his second-straight hundred-plus game in a string of record regular-season performances that would not end until it reached thirty-one.

After Washington State fell 27–3, it was Wisconsin's turn. The Buckeyes shut out the Badgers 24–0, and all Archie remembers about his 169-yard performance is one play.

"Corny Greene called a play, I guess it was an audible, and nine players went one way and he and I went the other."

The string of easy triumphs continued: It was 37–7 against Indiana, 60–0 over Northwestern, 30–0 vs. Illinois, then 35–0 over Michigan State.

"That was a sweet victory. We were thinking about how they had upset us the year before."

The Buckeyes put it all together again the following week against Iowa, and Archie broke his own single-game rushing record: He accumulated 94 yards in the first period alone and went on to pile up 246 yards as the Buckeyes rolled over the Hawkeyes, 55–13.

"That game proved to me that you can never tell ahead of time how you're gonna do once the game starts. In practice that week I thought all of us were taking Iowa pretty lightly, but once we took the field we couldn't do anything wrong. As for the record, I didn't know anything about it, but late in the third quarter Coach Hayes was sending Elmer Lippert into the game to take my place, but Elmer asked the coach to let me stay in because I needed just a couple of yards to break the record. So the coach told me to go back in for a couple of plays. It seemed like the guys on the team really wanted me to get the record. It didn't matter to me."

That victory left the Buckeyes with a 9–0 record. Nine victims had scored a total of but thirty-three points. There had been four shutouts, and no one had come within three touchdowns of the awesome Ohio machine.

Then came Michigan again, and the customary battle for Big Ten supremacy and the right to go to the Rose Bowl.

Woody Hayes left no doubt how he planned to attack the

game. Archie Griffin carried the football for the first three plays. He gained fifty-six yards during a drive that led to a field goal that put the Buckeyes in front early in the second period. On the drive later in that same period that resulted in Ohio's only touchdown, Archie accounted for forty-one of the fifty-five yards.

The second half was mainly Michigan. When Ohio State got the ball, it was all Archie. He toted it five straight times on the Buckeyes' first possession of the second half. Once Michigan gained a 10–10 tie in the final period, Archie got the call four times in succession. Archie's 163-yard performance got buried in the tangle of the 10–10 deadlock that brought on much controversy about which team should be voted into the Rose Bowl. Ohio State won the vote, and Michigan loyalists screamed.

"I kept thinking there wouldn't be as much excitement the second time around against Michigan, but it was the same thing all over again. You can play all season long, but the Michigan game is a totally different sort of thing. I remember taking some terrible hits. It was the worst beating I ever took. The Michigan wolfman, Don Dufek, was all over me. He played a terrific game. My knee was twisted. Some of our people said the Michigan guy did it deliberately, but how can you really say that? Both my hands were swollen nearly double their normal size. Someone hit me on every play, whether I had the ball or not. I got some yards, but I paid for every one of them. Maybe we should have felt all right after the tie, but in the locker room it was like we had lost. We had run over everybody, then had to settle for a tie. We just felt it was a tremendous opportunity for a perfect season and we had blown it, that's all."

Any frustrations the Buckeyes felt over the Michigan tie erupted in the Rose Bowl game against Southern Cal. In the 42–21 defeat of the Trojans, Archie Griffin gained 149 yards.

"We really took it to 'em. They had some great players like Haden and Davis and Wood and Swann and Cobb, but we were fired up because they had trounced us so badly the year before. We just had a lot to prove, and we went out and proved it. But for a long time that day, it looked like we'd fall on our faces again. We couldn't get untracked."

The score was deadlocked at the half, 14–14, and Archie, while he had gained sixty-one yards in fourteen carries, couldn't break a long one. The second time he handled the ball in the third quarter he fumbled, and Southern Cal's recovery led to the go-ahead score.

"I can't explain it, but when they went ahead of us, we all seemed to wake up all at once. We got two touchdowns in about three minutes, and from then on we had it together. We even completed some passes."

Archie had spurts of 25 and 47 yards and wound up with 149 yards and his first Rose Bowl touchdown.

The 1974 campaign was almost an exact replica of Archie's freshman season, except that the Buckeyes were 8–0 instead of 7–0 heading into the game against Michigan State. Archie had tied Steve Owens' intercollegiate record for consecutive 100-yard-plus games in the seventh game against Northwestern, and broken it with a 144-yard output the following week against Illinois. Both games were tremendously one-sided, as all the games that year had been.

Every year during Archie's career, there was a blotch on the Buckeyes' record. The first one of the 1974 season came in the 16–13 loss to Michigan State. National television viewers saw the controversial finish, the Buckeyes trying desperately to get off a final play that might have resulted in a touchdown and a victory, and the officials finally huddling in the locker room and deciding that the game was over and that Ohio State was not entitled to another play. It didn't matter that Archie produced 140 yards.

Two games later, it was the same script all over for the Ohio State-Michigan game. The winner would win the Big Ten championship and go to the Rose Bowl. The Buckeyes leaped on a pregame quote from one of the Michigan defensive players who said, "The only way Archie Griffin will get a hundred yards is over my dead body."

"It was in the papers but I didn't see the story. One of my professors told me about it, and our players were talking about it all week long. They said we'd just run every play at this guy and see what he said then. I guess our people talked to him quite a bit during the game."

Even though the Wolverines raced in front 10–0 in the first period, the Buckeyes made good on their vow to run Archie at the defensive end. In the first period Archie had gains of eighteen and fourteen yards.

"I guess I'll always remember that game as one of the real tests of the character of our club. Tom Klaban got a long field goal; then we got an interception that set up another field goal. Our defense did the job, and we got close enough for another field goal just before the half, and we were just one point behind. I didn't contribute much in the first half, but our defense held things together."

Archie Griffin's idea of not doing much: He carried sixteen times in the first half and gained eighty-nine yards.

Klaban got his fourth field goal early in the third period to make it 12–10 for Ohio State. The Buckeyes got across midfield just once more during the game, and then only to the Michigan forty-nine. Ohio's kicking and Michigan's lack of it sent the Buckeyes to their third straight Rose Bowl game. Tom Skladany had punts of sixty-three and fifty-five yards, and the Wolverines' field-goal kicker, Mike Lantry, missed attempts from fifty-nine and thirty-three yards, the last muff coming with just sixteen seconds to play.

"The Rose Bowl game was another of those nightmares. We thought we had it won when we went ahead 17–10 with about 6½ minutes left in the game. We had the lead and then lost it. Then, when we came back and got a touchdown and a field goal, we thought we could take it from there. But they put on a drive and stayed on the ground and ran right at us—that is, until that last play. We just let it slip away from us, that's all. We had no excuses."

The last play was a thirty-eight-yard pass from Pat Haden to

J. K. McKay, the coach's son, that left the Trojans one point behind. Then Haden passed for the two-point conversion that sent the Buckeyes down to a crushing 18–17 loss.

The Buckeyes' chances for an umblemished season had been ground into the turf against Michigan State in the ninth game of the regular season, and now they had to swallow another Rose Bowl defeat at the hands of Southern California. But Archie had so many awards he could not keep track of them. The highlight, of course, was winning his first Heisman Trophy.

In 1975, there were all the ingredients for the perfect season that had eluded Ohio State for so long. Hayes had his two hundredth college coaching victory behind him, his teams had won more games than any except those of Bear Bryant, his third book was selling well, and the old coach had made a rapid recovery from a heart attack. Starting his silver anniversary season, Woody had thirty-nine lettermen returning, and despite heavy losses in the line, none could doubt that this would be another banner year. It was no secret that the first four games would determine the success or failure of the season.

Ohio State opened against Michigan State, and the Buckeyes won it, 21–0. Archie said they were fired up because of the controversial ending to the game against the Spartans the previous season.

"The next week we played Penn State, and they played us tough. I'll always remember that game because I caught a pass at a real good time. I didn't catch that many passes, so maybe that's why I remember it."

It came in the final period, with Ohio trying to protect a 10–9 advantage. Woody Hayes is not what you'd call an advocate of the forward pass and often has said that there are three things that can happen to a football when you put it into the air, and two of those things are bad.

It started out like a typical Ohio State drive. The Buckeyes started from their twenty. They got to their thirty-two, but it was third and eleven for a first down.

"Corny called a pass, but I wasn't the primary receiver. I forget who was supposed to get the ball, but I got around a linebacker and got down the right sidelines and all of a sudden there was the football. I made a dive for it and got it and from then on we perked up."

The gain was good for twenty-three yards. Woody didn't chance another pass and alternated Archie and his big fullback, Pete Johnson, for nine plays until Johnson crashed in for the touchdown that put the contest out of reach.

It was Archie who broke open the North Carolina game the following week. Ohio State held a 12–0 half-time lead, but the Tarheels drew within five on the first drive of the second half. Then it was Griffin over right guard for seven, Griffin around right end for twenty-two, Griffin outside right tackle for fourteen. Pete Johnson rumbled the final yard. Archie helped set up two more touchdowns, and Ohio State prevailed, 32–7, for its third straight victory.

"All of us were scared even to think about going undefeated because we had messed it up three straight years. Besides, we had to play UCLA on the West Coast and it was a night game and it happened right at the time when all of us were really cramming for exams. I remember all of us had to take our books with us. It seemed like game time would never get there. We just sat around the hotel all day. I tried to take a nap, but I couldn't sleep. I spent most of the time in the bathroom, as usual.

"I wasn't very effective in the first half. I fumbled once, and they got the first touchdown. But Corny Greene had another great game, and our defense stuck 'em pretty good."

Archie's personal standards for his own production were so high by this time that he considered a 70-yard, 12-carry output in the first half not particularly effective. The second half was more of the same, Archie winding up with 160 yards and his team with a 41–20 victory before another national television audience.

The Buckeyes blanked Iowa and Wisconsin, holding both foes scoreless while running up 105 points. Purdue went down 35–6, and Griffin broke Ed Marinaro's intercollegiate rushing record for career yardage.

"I didn't know about it but people started talking about it and they wanted me to break the record at home rather than on the road at Purdue. But the players said, 'Let's do it now,' so that's when it happened."

No one would accuse Ohio State of pouring it on by leaving Griffin in the Purdue game. Archie didn't get his hundred yards until the score already was 35-6, and it was later in the final period when Hayes was persuaded to let him stay in long enough to establish an all-time major-college rushing record. It wasn't a back-door gainer that did it, rather a twenty-three-yard shot up the middle.

Woody Hayes rarely gives his squad days off during the season, but he announced there'd be no practice on Monday.

"Maybe he had second thoughts about it later on, 'cause we really came up flat against Indiana. They gave us a good game. I don't know, but maybe we were subconsciously already looking forward to the final game, with Michigan. I know we'd already worked against some of the Michigan plays."

Indeed, the Hoosiers played tough, fighting back from a 17-0 half-time deficit and moving to within three points before Ohio State seized control in the final period. Archie carried half a dozen times during a drive that was stymied by a Johnson fumble at the Indiana 1-yard-line. The Buckeyes got the ball right back on an interception, and Archie quickly bolted up the middle for 13 and then dashed around end for 4 more to set up the insurance score. Total yardage that day: 150 in 28 carries.

Illinois fell the following week, 40-3, but lived up to the name "Fighting Illini" for two periods, trailing at the half, 10-3, as Griffin scored the lone touchdown on a thirty-yard spurt up the gut.

"I have to laugh when I think back on that game. Coach Hayes didn't yell at us at half time, although he had reason to. We were okay in the second half, though. Corny Greene completed three straight passes, and someone remarked that it was the first time Ohio State ever even *threw* three passes in a row, not to mention completing them. I even caught three passes myself that day, and that was as many as I had caught the whole season before. I think we completed nine out of thirteen passes that day, and everyone was kidding that maybe it was an all-time record. It wasn't, though. Someone checked it out."

For Archie it was a fairly typical day, with 127 yards on the ground. That made 30 straight games of at least 100 yards rushing.

It was an emotion-packed scene the following Saturday in the jam-packed gray horseshoe along the banks of the Olentangy River in Columbus, Ohio. It not only was the windup against Michigan, with the customary marbles at stake, but it was also the final home game for Archie Griffin and twenty other Ohio State seniors.

"It's one of those days I'll never forget. They introduced all the seniors, and we were all pretty choked up, I guess. I know I was, because I was so grateful for all that had happened to me. I remember praying before the game, not to get a hundred yards or anything like that, but I asked God to help all our guys play up to their potential so we wouldn't disappoint the coach, the fans, or ourselves. I just wanted us to do our best."

It was not all that different from the dozens of other games Archie had played in front of the hometown fans. He got the Buckeyes started on their first scoring drive by breaking free for twenty-one yards. He squirted free on a nineteen-yard touchdown run in the second period and caught a pair of key passes. When the Gophers staged a mild flurry in the third period to make the score 17–6, Greene handed the ball to Archie four times in a row. It was Griffin who almost single-handedly ran the drive, gaining fifty yards en route to the touchdown that made the fans settle down more comfortably in their seats.

"Coming off the field when they sent someone in to replace me, I really had a queer feeling. I was happy, but at the same time I was sad. It was all I could do to keep from crying. As soon as the game was over, I prayed. Of course, I did that after every game, but I remember giving thanks for so many blessings I had during my career. The people had been tremendous to me and my family, and I was more grateful for that than for any of the honors or stuff like that."

Archie and his teammates headed into the annual Michigan confrontation with a perfect 10–0 record and the No. 1 ranking in the nation.

"It was a typical Michigan-Ohio State game. They absolutely killed me up there. They just about killed all of us. I didn't think I'd ever experienced hard hitting like I had in those earlier Michigan games, but this one was unbelievable."

The Buckeyes began the classic in near-freezing weather, as if they'd run the Wolverines right out of their huge stadium in front of 106,000 fans—most of them rooting for Michigan. On Ohio's first possession, the Buckeyes consumed some 9 minutes, 63 yards, and went in front 7–0. Archie Griffin carried the ball on 7 of the 15 plays, gaining 28 yards.

Archie would just as soon forget the rest of the game. He netted only 18 yards the rest of the day, three times was thrown for losses, and once lost the ball on a fumble. On this cold afternoon, another Griffin rescued the Buckeyes. Raymond, two years Archie's junior, got into the Michigan backfield repeatedly and three times spilled quarterback Rick Leach for losses. And once the Buckeyes tied the score 14–14 with but three-eighteen to play, it was Raymond Griffin who intercepted Leach's pass and returned it twenty-nine yards to the Michigan three-yard line. Johnson burst in for the winning touchdown, and Buckeye fans confirmed their reservations for Pasadena for the fourth straight year. Archie's amazing string of hundred-yard games was over. The Wolverines restricted him to a net of forty-six yards.

"But they couldn't stop the other Griffin," he said.

On January 1, the team Ohio State had thrashed by twenty-one points stopped every one of the Buckeyes.

The final score—UCLA 23, Ohio State 10—does not indicate the decisiveness with which the Bruins dispatched the Buckeyes. The Ohio State players were outplayed, and its coaches were outcoached by Dick Vermeil and his staff. Following the game, Hayes stalked off the field and locked himself, staff, and players away from the media people. There were bitter attacks against him for his gross lack of sportsmanship. Even the diehard loyalists had difficulty apologizing for him. Woody never would apologize for himself. The president of Ohio State University made a lame attempt but came up short of an attack. The Big Ten made a halfhearted effort. And Archie, given a year or more to think about it, still could not come up with strong criticism of his mentor and friend:

"I wish Coach Hayes would have said something, anything, but he chose not to, and that's his privilege, I guess. It's hard for me to be mad at him for things he's said or things he hasn't said, like in this case. No one but the players who play for him can possibly understand his disappointment. Outside of my own daddy, he's the hardest-working man I've ever met. He works from early morning to late at night, seven days a week, and I guess maybe he doesn't think of a single thing except football and winning. I know if we'd been able to win that game, we'd have continued to be ranked No. 1 in the country, and I'm sure he'd have been elected Coach of the Year. It was his twenty-fifth year of coaching at Ohio State and, well, it just had to mean everything in the world to him. And it all went up in smoke because we came up flat and played such an awful game. Still, I wish he would have said something. But he didn't. And that's Woody."

So, why couldn't Ohio State handle the team it had practically manhandled a few weeks before?

"It's a crazy thing to try to explain, but I guess we just didn't take the game seriously enough. We practiced with enthusiasm, but I think everyone was thinking about what we'd do after practice was over. The coaches kept telling us this would be a different UCLA team than the one we beat before. They kept pounding that into us, but I guess it just didn't soak through.

"We had won eleven in a row, and I guess we just took them for granted and figured they'd be No. 12. We just weren't serious enough about our preparation. We weren't mentally ready. We weren't tough enough. We controlled the game for a long time, but we didn't score when we had chances. I think we had the ball almost all the time in the first quarter (twelve minutes, eleven seconds to two minutes, forty-nine seconds for UCLA, and the Bruins had the ball only nine minutes, eight seconds in the entire first half), but we just piddled away our chances. By the time we realized we were in trouble, it was too late. You just can't turn things around automatically. There's no switch you can flick and make things happen like magic. Or if we had switches, so did the UCLA players, and theirs had been turned on a long time before ours had, maybe ever since we beat 'em 41–20. They just cared more than we did. I know that sounds horrible, but I think that's the honest truth."

The record shows that Ohio State got inside the UCLA thirty-five-yard-line four different times and put only three points on the board in the first half. Griffin accounted for seventy yards. One Ohio State drive was halted by two consecutive penalties, another by a fumble. Later, the UCLA quarterback, John Sciarra, would say, "We knew when we were down by only three points at the half that we had 'em."

They more than the Buckeyes. The Bruins tied the score on their first possession of the third period and went ahead on the next. Before the third period was over, they had taken complete command of the game and led, 16–3. The Buckeyes made one last flurry and drew to within six, but UCLA answered that touchdown with still another score.

Perhaps that was the pivotal part of the game. It was the part that caused some of the Ohio State fanatics to prove that they really do rate football ahead of God, home, and country. There was plenty of time remaining when Craig Cassady, son of an Ohio State Heisman Trophy winner twenty-one years earlier, intercepted a UCLA pass, and Ohio State got possession at the enemy's thirty-five yard line.

Quarterback Greene, who had passed successfully half a dozen times in twelve tries, passed on first down, but UCLA intercepted. Ohio partisans called it a panic call. But Ohio's defense stiffened, and UCLA relinquished the football once more. There was still enough time for the Buckeyes to extract a victory. Greene scrambled for eleven, and Archie got a yard to the Ohio forty-yard-line. On second down and nine yards to go, Greene passed again. Again, the Bruins intercepted. Two plays later they had their insurance touchdown, and for the third time in four seasons Ohio State's Rose Bowl hopes came crashing down on the turf in Pasadena. Archie had ninety-three yards, but a third Rose Bowl setback.

The explanation by Archie that perhaps UCLA's players simply cared more, and Woody's lack of explanation didn't satisfy some of the Buckeye fans. A popular rumor soon made the rounds around Columbus: The story was that Cornelius Greene had "thrown" the game. The most lavish figure thrown about amid the Buckeye madness was that Corny netted a cool fifty thousand dollars for himself.

"I heard all that stuff when I got back to Columbus after the game," Archie said. "I came right home because I had hurt my wrist and I had to get some treatment. Corny went on to Honolulu to get ready for the Hula Bowl game, and so he didn't hear the rumors until later. When I finally told him about them, he was really hurt. He didn't even want to come back to Columbus. I mean ever. Some people were putting out stories on the street that Corny was dealing in drugs, and somebody even told Pete Johnson the police were gonna plant some dope in Corny's apartment and then bust in there and arrest him. It was just terrible. I couldn't believe people would even think those things. When I finally talked with him after I went to Hawaii, he was in a terrible state of depression."

"After all, he was the same guy who led our teams to a ton of victories. He was a good runner, a pretty good passer, he showed great leadership, the guys believed in him, and he's a great human being. Now, Corny's different than I am. He's flashy. I'm conservative. He likes fancy things and all that, but until we lost that one big game everyone thought, 'Well, Corny Greene's just a flashy guy,' and no one said any more than that. Then one defeat, and some people start saying he took a lot of money to throw a football game. It's ridiculous. It's more than that. It's criminal even to think a thing like that of him, or anyone else on our team."

Even the Jack Armstrong type like Archie Griffin is aware of pot smoking and a certain amount of drug activity among some athletes.

"Hey, I'm not blind. Some of my friends smoke marijuana, and some of them mess around with other stuff. But when I'm around, they know not even to ask me. I don't have to do stuff like that to get along with people. They can like me for what I am. If some people wanna think I'm square, I can't help it, but if I have to deal with that stuff to be hip, then I'll just be square.

"And all those stories about guys getting big deals to play football. I've heard all that stuff. I went to Ohio State to get a good education and to play football. My football ability is what got that education for me, but I went to class and got it. All the other things that happened to me, the honors and the awards and all that, they're like bonuses. If I don't make it all right in pro ball, I believe I can fall back on my education and I won't starve. Someone asked me one time if I think Coach Hayes thinks as much of me now, because my career in college is all over. I really think he does, because all along I know he has cared about me as a human being."

While one cannot ask Woody Hayes to compare his feelings for one player against perhaps as many as a thousand he has tutored in his many seasons at Ohio State, it is apparent the old fellow has very special feelings about Archie Griffin. "He's the finest player and the finest young man ever to play for me," he says of Griffin.

Hayes gives Rudy Hubbard credit for doing most of the ground work with Archie but was quick to add, "I worked darned hard on

it, too. Someone had already done a good recruiting job on him—
I mean another school—because Arch had pretty much set his
sights on a smaller school. So that was the first obstacle we had to
overcome.

"But Arch was easy to talk to. There was obviously so much
quality there within the Griffin home. Over the years, you know,
I've made a great study of the home life of youngsters. Home life
is so important, and Archie's is so good. It's as good as any I've
ever heard of and the minute you walked into that home you
could spot two things: One, the youngster is the center of it, and
definitely wanted; secondly, discipline is good.

"Arch will tell you without hesitation that his father is the
greatest man in the world. And that's important, and it's unfortu-
nate that not too many young people feel that way these days.
The Griffins are good, solid, dependable, middle-of-the-road people. That's why I could see right away that Arch would be good in
politics. When he came here I made him promise me he'd get a
law degree. And I'm gonna hold him to that promise, too.

"If you study the history of the world, as I have, you'll find our
revolution was the only really successful one, because it never got
out of the hands of the moderates. You have to have moderate
people to keep things on the right track. Arch and all the other
members of his family have this great quality.

"Their home life is just without parallel. You know, this is why
I can't stand this women's lib thing, women wanting to leave the
home and all that. I'll tell you it just doesn't work. Right off you
could see all these good things in the Griffin home, and you could
see something else, too. All truly great athletes have an inner
confidence. Great athletes frequently are a little bit disliked by
their peer group, but this has never been true with Arch. I've
never once seen him do or say a single thing that would show ego-
tism or selfishness. But he has great confidence.

"Kids can spot those things, too, and right away they liked him.
They just had to. There's nothing phony about him. Blacks and
whites alike loved him instantly, and he and Brian Baschnagel,

whom we got here at the same time, did more to bring about understanding on our team than I could ever tell you. Both of them have this great depth, and so they instantly became the leaders of the squad. They didn't do it by yelling and screaming and jumping up and down, but just by doing their jobs well and by being great human beings. Neither one ever disappointed me. Not once in four years."

Like all coaches, Woody has had disappointments over the years. When he took over as coach at Ohio State in 1951, the place had become known as the graveyard of coaches. When his first team suffered three losses and two ties in the Big Ten, there was an immediate cry for his scalp. He had some trouble gaining control of the squad. Some of his players didn't accept his stern methods.

"Let's just not talk about that. Some people are easier to handle than others, and some come here from a better set of home circumstances. Sure, some kids have disappointed me. Who was it who said, 'Show me a hero and I'll write you a tragedy'? Who was that, anyway? I forget now.

"But I talked these things out with Arch, because it was obvious he'd be a star wherever he went and he'd have some difficult things to handle. He was a gifted young man, a touchdown kind. He just got touchdowns, that's all. It was obvious he'd be a star wherever he went. The only question was how soon. So we talked about some problems that sometimes fall upon those who attain stardom. I cited examples who've had the great college or pro careers, then who went downhill. That's why I stressed the education part with Arch. Of course, I do it with all young men—that's part of the script, you know, but it's a good one and it's right.

"But I really hammered at those points with Brian and Arch, because they were obviously unique. They were better athletes, better students, and they were better human beings. They were just in a class by themselves, and it was important for them to realize that they had to get a good education in order to realize their full potential. And with Arch, I had to sell him on the idea that he could come to Ohio State and play. Even though he had this great ability and confidence, he'd been told so many times that he'd get lost here, that he'd never play here, that I believe for a short time even Arch had some doubt about it."

Woody's critics have hinted over the years that the grizzled and often cantankerous old fellow will take the bows when things go well and distribute blame generously when they don't. But he was quick to credit not only one of his assistant coaches but also an old friend for helping persuade Archie Griffin to stay home to play his college football.

"His high school coach, Bob Stuart, and I had been in graduate school together right after World War II. He's quite a bit younger than I am, but we became good friends. When I'm trying to recruit a young man, the first person I seek out is his coach. I can learn a lot that way. A coach can tell you about whether a player has talent, whether he's unselfish, whether he's a leader or easily swayed, whether he has confidence and character. Besides, Stuart always turns out good teams, and Archie had been a kingpin for him. Bob was extremely proud of Arch, and I think down deep inside he wanted him to go where he'd not only play but also where he'd get a lot of attention."

Woody claims he was never concerned about Griffin's size.

"We proved years ago with Hopalong Cassady that size isn't the most important factor. Hoppy was only about 155 pounds when he came to us, but he had talent, and on top of that he had those great instincts that you simply cannot teach a young man. Arch had 'em too, only more of 'em."

In four seasons at Ohio State, Archie Griffin never missed a football game. He was repeatedly banged up. He quickly became a target, and every opponent figured the same way: Get Griffin out of the game and you've stopped the Ohio State offense. In his final two seasons, Archie rarely practiced as did the other players. He'd get so roughed up on Saturdays he'd spend a day or two on the training table getting the bumps and bruises tended to, then he'd jog lightly through the workouts the rest of the week to save himself for game days.

"Great conditioning is what kept Arch from getting seriously hurt. Lesser players, people with less character, would have been out of it. But Arch has always been a great believer in physical fitness. He could play a ball game with a week's notice twelve months out of the year. If I said, 'We're going to Russia to play,' he'd be ready because he never gets out of shape. He has great muscular control and better moves than the average player.

"Lots of people underestimate his speed, but it's there. He has wonderful quickness, too. You know, there's a big difference between sheer speed and quickness, but Arch has both of them. The main thing he has over other backs, though, is this tremendous ability to see the entire field. A good automobile driver does the same thing. Back in 1924, my uncle taught me that when he let me drive his old Dodge. You have to have anticipation and the ability to see everything that's going on. Arch always could see the whole field. You can't teach that."

Like Griffin's high school coach, Woody Hayes makes no claims about having taught Archie Griffin a whole lot.

Woody recalled the North Carolina game in Archie's freshman year, the time Archie forgot his helmet.

"I kidded him about it later and he said he just couldn't believe he was going in. He's so doggone humble. And let me tell you, his humility isn't the fake kind. It's real. A couple of times I actually stumbled over him going out of the locker room. I'd be looking ahead and everyone else would be dashing out onto the field and there'd be Arch, kneeling down and praying. But never once did he try to thrust his religious beliefs onto anyone else. But I'll guarantee you it rubbed off. That's why the kids liked him so much. His behavior and moral standards are higher than most kids', but even the kids who might not be believers never resented Arch. He has a certain way he lives his life, and it comes shining through every day."

It's been said of Woody Hayes that if you ask him for the time of day, he may tell you how to make a watch. When he speaks, he does so with great flourish and fervor and gets audiences to a point where if they are not quite ready to walk on water, they at least believe Woody can do it. Not infrequently, even at important recruiting sites before large groups, Hayes won't actually touch on the game of football. Instead, he'll talk about history, the changing social climate, and the problems that confront mankind.

"Young people today are much more difficult to coach, there's no question of that. There's been a tremendous breakdown in our morals. Our society has changed. We have so much domestic strife. Lots of kids, well, they just don't have any morals. They just live for today and think nothing of tomorrow. And that, my friend, goes right back to ancient times, when it was a case of 'Eat, drink, and be merry, for tomorrow we may die.' It may sound a little strange, but both Arch and Brian fit right into today's society without really belonging to it. They're with it, but not of it.

"No matter how a person may lack character and morals, that person will always look up to and admire the person who really has those great qualities. There may be a tinge of resentment, but that's just the lesser person's own dissatisfaction with himself coming through. And he may not confess it to you up front, but down deep inside he has a great feeling for that other person with the good qualities. It's what he'd really like to be. And that's why Arch was so important to us, not just when he was on the field doing something with the football, but as an all-around human being."

Coach Hayes said he noted an almost immediate change in the Ohio State squad once Griffin and Baschnagel joined the Buckeyes. And during Archie's last 2½ years in school, many members of the team got seriously involved in community work. It began at a banquet before Archie's second Rose Bowl appearance. The president of the University of Southern California rose to speak.

He said he could not know for certain whether his school would win the Rose Bowl game the following day, but he was sure that on the following day, quarterback Pat Haden would be back in the inner city of Los Angeles working with young people. Hayes recalled what happened after Ohio State's 42–21 victory:

"First, we all got down and said a prayer, giving thanks. When it was all over I said, 'Fellows, there's something I want to talk with you about when we get back home. I'm not gonna talk any more about it today, but we owe somebody a lot for this great victory today, and it's time we all started paying back.'

"When we got back, I suggested that members of our team get involved with our community. And from that time on, we sent our young men to inner city schools and churches and Scout packs and you name it, and the response was amazing. Of course, Arch was more in demand than the others. He'd stay on and on with the kids. Even after speaking, he'd go onto the playgrounds and play pickup games with the kids. He'd help them in the classrooms and help them if they had personal problems. He's just one of a kind."

Randy Gradishar remembers the effect Archie Griffin had on the Ohio State team. Gradishar, now a stickout linebacker with the Denver Broncos, played two seasons with Archie and twice won All-America honors for himself:

"He came there when we were coming off a 4–6 season, and that just isn't acceptable at Ohio State. The fans weren't happy, the coaches weren't happy, and the players didn't seem to have it together. The minute Archie joined the squad he had a positive effect on all of us. He's just super, that's all. He's the happiest human being I've ever known. You'll look all your life and you'll not find a better human being. He's a real winner and he's the guy who made Ohio State a winner again."

Gradishar, like Archie Griffin, made a decision to accept Jesus Christ as Savior while a student at Ohio State and he, too, had tremendous impact on others. And their old coach is quick to tell about them when he's out recruiting.

"I stress education when I'm recruiting because we want to produce people who will be contributing members of society. A lot of great words have been written by great people, and every time I read, I find something that's useful in my life or something I think can be useful to others. I like to see our people leave here and go out and help make the world a better place for the generations to come. Some folks say that's corny and a lot of bunk, but it's true. The football will take you only so far. Sometime later on you have to quit that and go on to something else. You can't play forever.

"And this is the very thing that crushes so many people. There's a story, and I ran onto it, believe it or not, in Michener's new book. And yet I had read it out in the Pacific during the war. It had a great impact on me back then and it still does. It was written by Irwin Shaw, and it's called 'The Eighty-yard Run.' The story is that this fellow breaks into the starting lineup as the result of this eighty-yard run he made in a scrimmage.

"He made the team then, but from then on everything in his life was downhill. That one run was the climax of his life. Now, twenty years later, after he had lost his wife, who had been his schoolgirl sweetheart, he was back selling suits in a store near the campus. So one day he went down to the practice field and tried to make that eighty-yard run again. A couple of kids were sitting by the sidelines, and this coed and her boyfriend looked up at him. He was kinda sheepish and said in a sort of guilty way, 'I played on the team here twenty years ago.'

"That's the tragedy of the story—that run was it for him. Everything was over and done with after that. And it can be that way so easily for people in sports. It happens even to the great ones. And that's the greatest tragedy in coaching, to see someone miss the wonderful opportunity of an education and a better way of life. But the greatest reward in coaching, more than any victory you might achieve, is an Archie Griffin. Just to know that you may have had some slight influence on a life like that, well, it's just stimulating, that's all. I've always regarded myself as the luckiest man in the world because of the people I have had with me, players and coaches. And I've had great players, not just here but at Miami and Denison and New Philadelphia High School.

"I am a pretty fair recruiter. I like to feel that I can get the best out of a football player. Maybe you'd call me a human engineer. I believe I can recognize talent, then use it."

In a comfortable situation there are moments of unusual candor with this man:

"I try not to be petty, but I am a petty person. And I have a terrible temper. And I'm a moody person. Moody people don't communicate too well. Another thing, as you get older, you make the horrible mistake of taking things for granted. You think people understand you when they really don't understand at all. You have a tendency to assume people know what you mean, and sometimes they don't. That's a lack of communication, pure and simple. The one mistake that I don't think I make is assuming that one kid is just like every other kid. They never are. They're all different, and they need different kinds of treatment and handling. I'm sure I've always been able to deal with people as individuals."

Woody Hayes had talked for hours about Archie Griffin, about himself, about his philosophy, his outlook on life. The hour was late. But there was a final question that had to be asked. It seemed valid, not disrespectful. After all, the relationship went back a quarter century, and he had spent time in the Diles' home in Middleport, Ohio, and eaten Mom's lemon pie and shared hours of nonfootball conversation with the people dearest to me. There really was no delicate way to phrase it, so it came out, "Why don't you quit, Woody?"

He looked almost hurt, then the words came slowly, almost in a pleading manner:

"What would I do, Dave? You see, this has been my whole life. I mean, all of it. I love it. I love the challenge. I love the fact that I'm busy. I love the fact that I'm never bored with it. Yet there are times when physically, you get tired, and I mean really tired.

You're taxed just about as far as you can go. I get up at five-thirty in the morning, and I don't get to bed until eleven or twelve at night, and I'm going hard most of the day."

Then he turned tough again and insisted on winding up the interview. It was late. The assistant coaches had left a long time ago. But there was nothing more to ask the man. He looked tired. The hair was gray, almost white, and even though he had taken off some weight and was not as heavy as he had been, he still carried that paunch around the middle, and the omnipresent jowls sagged a bit more. But the man had jowls when he came to Columbus. He also had a jaw that jutted out in a defiant manner, and a finger that he pointed at you when he wanted to add extra authority to whatever he was saying. And these things had not changed at all. After he turned out the lights, we walked together to the parking lot, and before he turned to head home he said: "You know, Dave, if you write a hundred books in your lifetime, you'll never write one about a finer human being than Archie Griffin."

Wayne Woodrow Hayes, unpredictable if nothing else, had been charming and gracious and hospitable. At other times he had indeed been petty, temperamental, moody, and uncommunicative. At one time he was the only Big Ten coach who refused to take part in a preseason television special. His violent temper had erupted into a wild torrent of exhibitionism on the field at Michigan one chilly afternoon when a critical call went against his team.

Not many weeks later, this same man spoke out about the increasing problem of crowd control and fans' behavior. In a speech that was impassioned if not volatile, he alluded to the increasing bent for violence across the land, the evils of a permissive society, and the need for immediate curbs. Later that year, he would try to beg off a network television interview he had promised the week before the Ohio State-Michigan showdown. He consented reluctantly but only after a lengthy exchange on the responsibilities of the media against those of NCAA schools, the preparation time required for such an important game, and the money paid competing schools by the network. He finally agreed to hold still for ninety seconds, and the cameras had rolled to that point when it seemed logical, if not reckless, to go back to Coach Hayes' statements about crowd behavior and to ask him about his own sideline behavior at the earlier Michigan game. It was the fire that lit the celebrated Hayes fuse.

"That's terrible journalism, just terrible. That's in the past. I knew you'd bring it up, and I don't like it a bit. You're not doing your job."

It did no good to talk about journalistic integrity, because there is none so blind as he who will not see, and none so deaf as he who will not hear. He strode from the room. Long after the interview was played, in its entirety, and after Ohio State had beaten Michigan, gone to the Rose Bowl, and all that, Archie Griffin would nearly double up in laughter when the story was relayed to him.

"I can just see all that happening. That's the coach, all right. He can be the most charming, the warmest guy in the world, if he wants to be that way. But he gets so wrapped up sometimes in his own little football world that, well, he just can't see anything else. But I don't believe he holds many grudges, and I doubt if there are many people he really dislikes, down deep. I know there are things that stick with him, but he's pretty quick to forgive and forget."

Archie said he figured out quickly when he got to school that the coach would be firm but friendly, and in four years there was just one incident that might be termed challenging. It came when Griffin, Neal Colzie, Cornelius Greene, and Steve Luke each got a car prior to Archie's junior season.

"He walked right up to me and said, 'Your car is legal, isn't it?,' and before I had time to say anything more than 'Yes' he pointed his finger at me and said, 'You know, I'm going to check up on it, don't you? I'll have investigators come in and check everything out, just to be certain. I don't want any trouble over cars.' Well, he kept on all of us and made sure the papers were all right and that our families had arranged financing for the cars. My dad signed for me, because he believed all of us should have transportation, and he worked hard to get it for us.

"My older brothers got their cars the same way. I guess that's one of the reasons he's worked two and three jobs for all these years. His family always is his first consideration, and he wants things to be good for us."

The Griffin goodness sometimes turns folks off. When word first reached Columbus that there'd be a book on Archie, some bigot wrote a nasty card suggesting a racist title for the work. Of course, there was no name at the bottom of the card.

Steve Harms might have been turned off, too, except that he got to see the goodness up close. Harms was doing the six and eleven o'clock reports on Columbus television, and the city had not provided an easy transition for him. He had come from a city of much greater size, if no more sophistication. The town he left was occupied by four professional sports franchises, all of them operating if not performing at a major-league level.

"Columbus took a lot of getting used to. From a media standpoint, and from the standpoint of the fans as well, it's strictly an Archie Griffin-Jack Nicklaus town. It seems like these two guys have been, well, security blankets for the whole city. They've already been canonized. I thought surely there must be something else going on here besides Ohio State football and Jack Nicklaus's golf scores.

"But it's that way, and there isn't a thing you can do about it. Ninety per cent of the readers and viewers just don't give a hoot about anything else. They just don't care if someone at some other college scored nine touchdowns and ran for six hundred yards. It's what Archie does that counts, and now that he's graduated, the media and the fans concentrate on the team and all the while keep an eye out for another big hero.

"When a Columbus writer goes to cover a major golf tournament, his basic function is to write as if it's a one-man golf tournament. He's there to cover Nicklaus, and anything else is incidental. Oh, Tom Weiskopf sneaks in there now and again and gets some ink. But primarily, it's Jack Nicklaus.

"I just couldn't believe the constant attention given these people. I'd never been in a situation where the whole town is caught up in one or two things like that. I got here right at the start of the Archie thing, and I was absolutely staggered by it. His every move, every word was recorded as if all of it someday would go into a time capsule. You find yourself starting to dislike these people, and for no reason at all."

Archie had just finished his sophomore season when Harms approached him at a banquet about doing an interview.

"I actually interrupted him, because I had to make a determination on how long to keep my film crew. I assumed maybe he'd tell me he could work in an interview after he made his talk at the banquet. I would have been well satisfied with that, and would have understood it. But he stopped right now and said, 'Fine, would you like to do it now?' There wasn't any hesitation and he didn't want to know what I was going to ask him, and he couldn't have been nicer nor more gracious. Over the next couple of years I got to know him much better, and I learned he's a dedicated, disciplined, down-to-earth guy with terrifically high morals. And I'd have to say he's done more good, more to influence not just his teammates and other students at the university, but also young people all over the place than any person I've ever met or heard of in sports. You just have to be better for knowing Archie. And you know what? After I spent some time around Jack Nicklaus, I found he's another tremendous person.

"It bothered me that so many people would have built-in excuses all ready just in case Archie didn't win the Heisman Trophy for the second time. He didn't need anyone to apologize for him. He'd never need an alibi, nor would he accept one for anything, on the field or off it. But some people were running scared when the time came for the voting in his senior year. They were ready to put the blame everywhere in the world.

"It wouldn't have been a national disgrace had he not won it. He'd already done more than most people ever do, and he'd won it once, and winning it twice had never been done anyway. I'd have to say the town didn't have a big-league approach to it, but Archie himself was class all the way. I'd bet my bottom dollar that if he hadn't won it, he'd be the first to congratulate the player who did. He was under the microscope more than any athlete I've ever seen, but I can't think of a thing he said or did that would cast him, his family, his team, his school, anything, in a bad light. Everyone knows he's a remarkable athlete, but I think he's even more remarkable as a human being."

Griffin himself was embarrassed a bit by the Heisman hoopla.

"Sure, I wanted to win it again. It'd be a big lie to say I didn't. But when they came out with those bumper stickers saying 'Thank You, Mrs. Griffin' and all that, it made me feel a little silly. Everybody was talking about winning the Heisman Trophy again. I don't go around reading articles about myself, but there was no way I could avoid what was going on. I can honestly say, though, that I didn't think I had any inside track on the award, and it wouldn't have torn my whole world up not to win it."

Archie handled his own success better than he did some other things he encountered on campus.

"College was a good time for me, but there's one thing that really disillusioned me, and that's the drug problem. And it's a real problem. Maybe I was a little blind to it all when I was in high school, even though I knew some people smoked marijuana and maybe some others took some pills. But when I got to college, I saw a lot more of that stuff."

Even on the football team?

"Sure, there are guys who drink and some guys who smoke pot, but I've never known anyone to get into the hard stuff, I mean pills and things like that. All that stuff has been offered to me, and people have told me how good it makes them feel. But I feel good all the time already, and I don't need anything else to make me feel good. I think life's a pretty good thing the way it is, and there is still another life waiting for those who serve the Lord. I get pretty concerned about the future of the world when I see some of the things that are going on.

"I just wonder where our country is heading. That's why I give my time to kids. I always will. Someone has to go out and tell them about the good things that are going on. Someone has to go out and prove to them that they don't need grass and pills and those other things. If they'll listen to Archie Griffin and if they'll believe Archie Griffin, then Archie Griffin is gonna talk to them and tell them the right way to go. It worries me that a lot of kids don't have any respect for older people. But I'm not that much older than some of those kids, so maybe they'll listen to me. When I think about it, the very best thing about being well known because of football is the good that I might be able to do because people will listen to me."

The requests from folks who wanted to listen to Archie during his college days were in the thousands. Every day there were requests for interviews, speeches, and picture-taking sessions. The man who had to separate most of them is Marv Homan. He graduated from the same university in 1948, had a brief fling in radio, then came back to the school in August 1949 and never got around to leaving. Homan is director of sports information at Ohio State.

"I've been through some All-American situations here because we've had our share of publicity and attention. And you have to consider that for a long time we've had a coach who makes news. But I've never known a person who handled the attention with more grace and humility than Archie Griffin. The total truth is, Archie had more attention than most of the other All-Americans put together."

There have been nearly forty All-Americans at Ohio State just since Homan's arrival. He said he never once saw Archie lose his cool.

"On the field, I've seen only the slightest show of emotion, and then when he'd drop a pass or miss a blocking assignment. Then he'd get mad briefly, but only at himself. He'd be rather sheepish, even remorseful, even then for losing his cool for half a second. But he was ideal under the most severe of circumstances away from the football field. I really couldn't begin to count the requests.

"Sometimes now I wish I had kept a running count, but I know the requests had to number in the thousands. If it wasn't a Cub Scout guy it was a contest winner, or a pumpkin queen, or the Kidney Fund or Heart Fund or some other group. I swear Ohio has them all. And Archie was asked to pose with every one of them. I'm sure he sat still for pictures having to do with nearly every part of the human anatomy, and posed with a queen representing every type of fruit and vegetable.

"And he was absolutely delightful every time. He never turned anyone down, and we were swamped. And this isn't counting the media. My assistant, Steve Snapp, and I would be almost apologetic when we'd call him with another request. But he never was upset with us, or at least it never showed. He was beautifully cooperative. He had only one rule: He wouldn't cut any classes for publicity. But he'd skip lunch."

It was not necessary for Homan to detail the sometimes selfish attitudes of the media. "Just one picture, please" turns into twenty, and a three-minute film segment turns into a documentary. A two-question interview becomes a serial.

"He was never late for an appointment and never broke an engagement. He was tolerant and considerate when many times the people on the other end weren't. Frankly, there were times when Steve and I wanted to throw up our hands and yell, 'Halt, that's enough, for God's sake.' But it was no use. Archie was forever smiling, and had we done something like that he probably would have gone ahead anyway. The networks and national magazines swooped down on him in great hordes, but he never lost his poise. And if he got upset by a single question, it never showed. He's just a beautiful human being, an almost unbelievable one."

It seemed like a job for a tightrope walker, balancing the

effervescent Archie and the irascible Woody. Homan said it wasn't all that much trouble.

"Like every job, this one has its difficult moments, but I love the university setting and the realism of the place. I love the Athletic Department. It has to be aggressive, competitive, and the relationship with the athletes and coaches is exciting. Sure, I've been provoked at Woody for the things he's done, or hasn't done in some cases. But they're isolated cases. He's real. He's not phony. The affection of his players for him is genuine. You ask any ex-player about him, and you'll find a warmth that you won't find by asking workers about former bosses. It's incredible. Now, I'm not accusing anyone of anything, but it's a fact that very few people know about the really fine things Woody has done. Not very many people know how generous and unselfish he is."

Homan told of the time the president of a major corporation asked Woody to speak to the annual national convention of the Boy Scouts of America. Woody accepted, and dazzled the audience. Many listeners, former critics, became disciples. The host handed Woody a check for five thousand dollars.

"What's this for?" Homan said Woody inquired.

The corporate big wheel explained it was an honorarium for doing the speech.

"I could never accept that," Woody is said to have protested.

The man then offered three thousand dollars, thinking that might be more in line with Hayes' customary fee. Again, Hayes turned him down, explaining that he expected nothing for speaking to such a fine group. The host insisted Woody take something. The coach thought a bit, then said "Well, I'm going to Colorado before long and I'd really like to have a pair of hiking boots."

And that's all he would accept for the appearance.

When one of his Big Ten coaching colleagues, Alex Agase— then at Purdue—heard the story, he told Woody when next they met, "You know, I always knew you were crazy, and this confirms it."

Homan told a story about an Archie Griffin speech that had much the same ring to it. It was Homan who approached Archie about speaking at Georgetown College in Kentucky. It's a Baptist-affiliated school, and Homan's daughter Jane was attending school there.

"I was a little hesitant about asking him, and I told him he need not feel any obligation. But right away, he was eager to do it. He didn't ask about a fee or anything. Now, he was appearing at a virtually all-white school where the audience, well, it might be a little more suspect than normal. He was a black kid, a two-time Heisman Trophy winner and the only one in history, and he went down there and spoke about his faith in God and how God had enriched his life and how the fullness of his home life had set him on the right path in life. What he did is overwhelm them. They gave him a standing ovation, and this is typical of the good that Archie has done since the day he came to school here."

Homan saw Archie lose his composure just once.

"He was giving his acceptance speech at the Downtown Athletic Club in New York after getting his first Heisman award. He was about three quarters of the way through it, and he started to introduce his family. He was telling what his family meant to him, and he simply got all choked up and cried."

Archie recalled that time and was almost apologetic for his failure to hold back the tears.

"It just got to me," Archie said. "Here I am up there getting an award that rightfully should be shared by not only my teammates, but also my family. They all put me there. And I just wish every young person could have looked into my heart and known what I was feeling as I stood there. With the type of home life my parents provided for me there's just no way I could turn out to be a really bad person."

Once Archie had won his second Heisman Trophy and had his college degree, the pressures increased. In May of 1976 at Capital University in Columbus there was a Conference on Crime, and the sponsors called on Archie. There were 9 people on the platform and maybe 250 people in the room. The keynote speaker at the morning session was an assistant attorney general of the United States, a fellow in charge of the Criminal Division of the Department of Justice.

Panelists included a chief of police, a judge, a woman from the Cincinnati Planning Commission, the chairman of the state Adult Parole Board, a former FBI agent, and a newspaper editor. Theirs was a common concern over the staggering increase in crime. The statistics had been particularly shocking to Columbus, a city that has taken great pride in once being selected by *Look* magazine as an All-American city. They would try to learn the why of those statistics, then come up with some ideas about solution and prevention.

Bill Gardner, an investigator with the prosecutor's office, said it was natural to ask Archie Griffin to take part "not just because he's a football player but because he's a concerned citizen and an outstanding public figure, and because he's one of the young people who can be used as an example for good."

The woman on the panel talked about having spent three years in Ethiopa. There, she said, some young men broke into a girls' dormitory in an attempt to assault the young women. The men never finished the assault but were brought to swift justice.

"They were hanged in public and left there for three days," she said. "Words were displayed, telling what they had done so the general public would be informed of the crime and the punishment. I never heard of any more assaults in the three years I was there."

She added quickly she was not advocating that type of punishment but said it seemed to be a deterrent. She went on to deplore the violence on television and the generally inaccurate portrayal of policemen.

The chief of police of Canton, Ohio, didn't once mention public hangings. Instead, he took off on judges, parole boards, and others in a system he said was "soft on criminals." He was particularly upset about the abuse policemen have to take.

The chap from the Ohio Adult Parole Board did not want the board abolished, as others suggested because of an alleged namby-pamby attitude toward criminals. But he admitted that changes should and would be made. He got pretty funny during his talk, and said what we're doing in prison now is taking a two-, three-, or four-time loser and making a hero out of him.

"The guy sits there and we're hearing his plea for probation and he has right there in his hand a grant for two, three, or maybe four thousand dollars either from the federal government or the state so he can go out of prison and get a college education. He's gonna get it all paid for by someone else. Now, I have two kids myself, and I'm gonna have to put them through college by myself. One of my kids said, half-kiddingly, that maybe the best thing for him to do was go out and commit a crime and get sent to prison so he can get his education paid for by the government."

The man's speech made Archie Griffin laugh. Archie's speech made everybody sit up and take notice. He was billed as "Archie Mason Griffin, athlete and civic leader." Barely out of college, he was both. The man who introduced Archie skimmed over his athletic accomplishments and talked instead about Archie's concern and commitment to his state and nation. That concern manifested itself in what Archie said:

"At various times of my life, in high school and college, I have been urged to get with the 'in crowd.' I had to be strong not to join the crowd sometimes. But I had a good enough home life so I was able to resist that kind of temptation. Lots of kids are in the 'in crowd' because they're on the outs with society. Their home life has been miserable and their parents haven't been able to get it together and they've had too much time alone, too much time without supervision, too much time to get in trouble.

"The Griffins are a busy family, and we leave no time for getting into trouble. Other kids were allowed to stay out late and run around, but we always had to be in at a certain time. There were no exceptions and no excuses. We had love, we had fellowship and a belief in God and the desire to do things together as a family.

"It's important for people to have things to do, to keep busy. When people have nothing to do, that's when they get in trouble. During my final years at Ohio State, I did some research work at the Ohio Workhouse. I met with a lot of prisoners, and I asked all of them why they were in there serving time. And a lot of them told me they got into crime because it was easy, because they knew the chances of getting caught weren't that great, and even if they did get caught their chances of being severely punished weren't great at all.

"The atmosphere is right for crime. Criminals know it's an easy route, pretty much, these days. Policemen's hands are tied, and crime really does pay. We have become too easy on criminals and everyone knows it, particularly the criminals. I sincerely believe we have to crack down, and I'm inclined to agree with the lady who talked about public hangings."

When Archie Griffin hit that line, it was all one could do to keep from falling out of the chair. But no one made a peep. He sounded more like General George Patton, and Archie's fervor was akin to that of the Bible-waving evangelists who used to bring their tents and posters to southeastern Ohio. Archie concluded on a ringing note:

"You know, when I was a youngster and I did something wrong, my mother didn't stop to have a hearing or a meeting. She just handed out the punishment. I've always remembered that. The punishment part stayed with me, I think that when you do something wrong, you should pay for it. Problems pretty much originate in the home, and in recent years we've let down in the home life department. Families don't do things together. Home life isn't as important, and when you have problems in the home you have to wind up with problems in the street. When you don't have discipline in the home, you don't have much of anything. Discipline isn't just punishment. It's love."

Archie folded the piece of paper on which he had written some notes for his speech. He sat down. The applause was deafening and went on for minutes. It was an incredible experience.

The judge had spoken about doubling the size of the police force, the chief had talk about judges being too lenient, someone else pointed out that laws have become less stringent, the parole guy blamed the bureaucracy, but Archie Griffin got right down to the root of the problem that confronts not just just Columbus, Ohio, but also every city and hamlet in the nation, indeed the world. He had dealt in common sense and talked about the human involvement in crime, and in crime prevention. And he was not yet twenty-two years old.

Bob Smith, the editor of the Columbus *Dispatch*, talked about what he called "Archie impact" in Ohio:

"There's no way to measure it. He's the perfect example. He's had a good, clean family life. His mother and father are more than willing to go out and tell how they've raised their children. We have a noninvolved society, but the Griffins are involved people. No one got a dime for appearing at this conference.

"When we asked Archie to take part, he said 'Yes' right away. He didn't even ask about a fee. And he wouldn't take anything. He's a law-and-order guy who knows right from wrong, and he feels a great responsibility. The fact that he has attained such fame in football makes more people listen to him. But you know, people would still turn him off if he didn't have something to say. I feel sorry for the ones who think of Archie as nothing more than a football hero. They're missing the real human being, and they're the losers because of it."

The prosecuting attorney of Gallia County, Gene Wetherholt, said the Archie impact will be felt for years to come.

"I used to think we could solve our problems with laws, but we have to solve them with people. Archie Griffin gives young people something to believe in, something to strive for, something worthwhile and lofty to believe in."

Tom DeLay of Jackson County hopes Archie can make more appearances before older people:

"The kids love him and look up to him, but he has great influence on older people, too. We have big problems not just because kids are less than we'd like them to be but also because we've failed as parents. Morally, we've given too many bad examples to our young people. We've let them make heroes out of the Yippies and hippies, and it's our fault some of them have turned out the way they have.

"It's disgusting that so many young people follow and believe in Charles Manson and Abby Hoffman and the other freaks. It's a national disgrace, but we have no one to blame but ourselves. With a few more people like Archie Griffin, though, we can turn it around. He's a man who has these ideals and principles and the ability to express them so beautifully. You listen to Archie Griffin and you know what he's saying is true and that it's coming right from his heart."

If law-enforcement people applauded what Archie said, it is just as certain that some militant blacks would not. But with Archie, it boils down to a matter of believing something and being willing to speak out about those beliefs.

"I know my beliefs aren't shared by everyone, but I have certain things I believe to be true, and things I believe in because of the way I was brought up. I have to be honest about my beliefs. I can't lie, can I?"

He not only cannot, but he also would not. But it is a persuasive argument, when someone cites statistics showing crime among blacks, and showing that blacks are most frequently victimized by crime, to point out that blacks are more culturally and economically deprived and that in some cases they are taking what they feel they have a right to own.

"I think I can understand the whole picture. At least I try to. But I've never felt any discrimination. Maybe some folks don't like me because I'm black, and maybe some folks have hated me and tried to discriminate against me. But I've never felt like a victim. I know someone will read that and say, 'Hey, how can he talk about it if he's never had it hurt him?,' and I can appreciate that. I know there has been a lot of discrimination and prejudice and bigotry down through the years, and it's still going on in lots of places. I know what my people have had to endure.

"But when I was growing up, I didn't look at things as black or

white or anything else. I looked at things as a person. Until I got
to college, I didn't understand how seriously some people take
this race thing. Our high school had a few racial problems, but I
think it was more a fad than anything else. There was an issue
once about some of the grades some of the blacks got, but it
wasn't an issue very long. There was some business about having
more black teachers and more black-oriented studies, but they
worked it out.

"I've always felt that if I apply myself, things will turn out the
way I want them to be. I don't like to make excuses for not doing
well, and I take it as a personal responsibility to do the best I can.
I feel black people have as much intelligence as anybody, and it's
been proved that a black man, given the same opportunity, can do
as well as anyone else. Some folks might say, 'Well, how many
blacks have become ambassadors, and how many blacks have become this and that,' but if blacks are given the same education
and the same background, they wind up at the same level as all
other people. It's just that I didn't have to fight any racial battles.
But that's not to say I don't appreciate the battles others have
fought in my behalf.

"Lots of blacks haven't had the same opportunities as whites.
And lots of people, black and white, haven't had the same chance
in life that Archie Griffin has had. But sometimes opportunity is
something you have to create for yourself. I don't think you can
sit around and wait for someone to hand it to you. You have to go
out and work hard and hustle and make things happen. I worked
hard in football and worked hard in the classroom, and I believe
that's why I've had a little bit of success. I look at Coach Hayes.
He recruits hard. He works hard. Parents can relate to him. Sure,
he gets good talent, but he works like the devil with that talent.
That's why Ohio State is good in football. It's no accident."

Archie and Woody, strikingly dissimilar in background, yet
remarkably alike in their thinking, advocates of the great American work ethic, believers in the theory that the harder you toil,

the luckier you get, law-and-order middle-of-the-roaders who believe only the moderates can save society from self-destruction.

Woody Hayes has been accused of living in the past, and he doesn't deny it altogether.

"We all do it, and it's not a bad thing. We all should make a more thorough study of history and we'd be a lot better equipped to handle today and tomorrow. We're in a state of constant change, and we've let some great opportunities get away from us because we've been asleep. We haven't been paying attention. That's why we have the decay we've had. That's why people are like they are today.

"We like to think of our All-Americans as the Jack Armstrong type with great principles and morals off the field to match their performance on the field. With Archie Griffin, you don't have to wish for that kind of combination. He's just loaded with tremendous qualities, and if we're to save the world, the Archie Griffins will have to do it for us. He's the best. There likely will not be another like him."

The time would come—and soon—when Archie would need all those qualities, and more.

# 2

## *Welcome to the Real World, Archie*

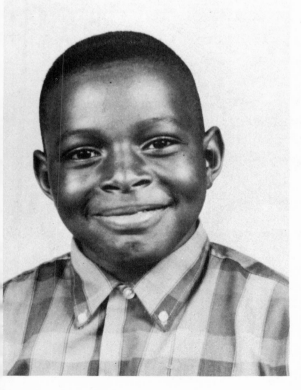

1. *Above,* The amazing
Griffins—Left to right:
James, Jr., Daryle,
James, Sr., Duncan,
Archie, Mrs. Margaret
Griffin, Raymond, Larry,
Crystal, and Keith.
2. *Left,* Archie—when he
was so fat his pals
called him "Tank" Griffin
—and he had to diet
to make the weight to
play elementary school
football.

3. Archie (middle, back row) when he played on a championship team in junior high school.

4. Archie (No. 35) carrying the ball for Eastmore High School.

5. Archie running on the track team at Eastmore High.

6. Archie taking a tumble during a wrestling
match at Eastmore High School.

7. Look out, here they come again! This is what Ohio State opponents had to face, with Cornelius Greene handing off to Archie Griffin, and Pete Johnson looking for someone to block.

8. This is the way Archie Griffin looked to most of Ohio State's opponents for four seasons. The side and rear views were most common, as in this action from the Illinois game in 1975.

9. It all started in the second game of Archie's freshman year, when he established a school rushing record against North Carolina. On this run he had Pagac (No. 80) and Bonica (No. 58) and France (No. 77) and Kregel (No. 63) and Hare (No. 18) and Keith (No. 4) out in front, forming a wall of blockers.

For twenty-one years of his life, Archie Griffin lived in a kind of isolation. From the time he first achieved a measure of stardom in high school, he heard only good things, saw only good writeups.

Columbus, Ohio, heaps lavish attention on its athletic heroes, and its stars get more than ample praise and protection. Not until Archie Griffin had twice won the Heisman Trophy as the nation's top collegiate football player, and not until he had been elected an All-American three times did he get his first taste of criticism. It was a rude welcome to the real world awaiting a young man who now would have to earn a living through his skills.

As it turned out, the criticism he got after winning an unprecedented second Heisman Trophy was just a taste. More criticism would follow quickly.

It was a curious coincidence that the author was sitting in a New York network television studio when a colleague unleashed the first barrage of criticism. Warner Wolf, appearing on ABC TV's "College Football Scoreboard" following the Saturday afternoon football games, questioned the wisdom of the Heisman voters. He suggested they had looked more at Archie's four-year record at Ohio State than at his performance in his senior year.

Wolf cited statistics showing that several other players outgained Griffin in the 1975 season.

Archie missed the show, since he was preparing for a banquet address at the time, but word was quickly sent to him that the selection was at least being questioned. When I asked Archie about Warner's criticism, his reaction was low-key:

"I'm sure the Heisman Trophy could have been awarded to several people. It isn't something you campaign for, except that every player works hard—and I believe every good player thinks about his team above himself. What campaigning you do, you might say, is with your performance on the field.

"I realize I was more fortunate than some because I played with an outstanding team and got a lot of national exposure. And the fact that I had won the Heisman Trophy the year before didn't hurt, I know. Now, I'm not saying I deserved the award more than others. But when they gave it to me, I didn't feel ashamed in taking it. In other words, I wasn't embarrassed.

"My selection had to make some folks unhappy, and I'm sure some other players were disappointed. I'd have been disappointed if I hadn't won it, although I know I could have taken it in stride."

Archie spent minutes avoiding a direct answer about the criticism on network television.

"Let's put it this way," he finally said in a near confrontation with the issue, "he had a right to criticize, and I guess I had a right to win it. But if you think I enjoyed the criticism, no way. I think there's something wrong with a person if he enjoys criticism. A good human being has to expect criticism and has to know how to handle it—but at the same time, criticism should be handed out in the right way."

As it turned out, that was just the beginning for the young man who had known nothing but praise.

The headline in the Columbus *Dispatch* read like this:

ARCHIE TACKLING A NEW POSITION

OSU STAR TO TOUR SCHOOLS

Shortly after he graduated from Ohio State University with a bachelor's degree in industrial relations, Archie took a temporary job with the Department of Education of the state of Ohio.

The state superintendent of schools, Martin Essex, had the program in mind even before Archie won the Heisman Trophy for the first time. Archie, he figured, would add a new dimension to the state's right-to-read program in the public schools.

It's a federally funded program, and Archie would be paid $125 a day. The arrangement was for Griffin to visit schools and speak to assemblies and meet with various groups in an effort to spur interest in reading among schoolchildren.

After all, educators generally agree that for some reason, Johnny can't read—and for that matter, neither can Jennifer. The old three-*r* system of readin', ritin', and 'rithmetic seems to have gone by the wayside. It would be Archie's job to generate some new enthusiasm for at least one of the *r*'s.

The Ohio Department of Education arranged for students to become "All-American Readers" by reading five books—and get an iron-on symbol for every five books read. After reading a hundred books, the student would receive a "touchdown" award.

Essex went through Coach Woody Hayes to get to Archie.

At about that same time, in the spring of 1976, some Archie supporters moved to have a street in Columbus, Ohio, named after their hero. The Columbus newspapers—the *Dispatch* and the *Citizen-Journal*—were deluged by mail. The suggestion became a public issue. There were more people for the proposal than against it, but the outpouring of protest was sufficient that the matter was quietly dropped some months later.

Not all the protest mail was from bigots. Some of it came from folks who simply thought that $125 a day was far too much money for a "jock" and folks who figured there were those who had earned a street-naming more than an Ohio State football player.

The bigots had their facts jumbled, as bigots almost always do. They insisted that Archie's money was coming from their tax dol-

lars. The money, in fact, came from The Right-to-read Special-
purpose Grant OEG-0-72-1576. Funds were allocated by Congress
for reading-improvement efforts in all fifty states.

Ohio came up with the Archie Griffin Reading Incentive As-
semblies.

Virginia Kunkle, the director of the Division of Educational
Redesign and Renewal in the Department of Education, is
credited with thinking it up. The state of Ohio was divided into a
dozen right-to-read areas, and Archie spent twenty days speaking
to students in Grades 5 through 8. He gave at least four speeches
a day.

Archie's net was $2,500—but bigots often can't multiply, either.
One letter-writer figured Archie's pay at $24,375.

Considering the uproar over Archie's "windfall," it seemed like
a good idea to follow him around for a while and check his effec-
tiveness.

On a day early in June, Archie was to speak to four schools in
Lorain, Ohio. Lorain is a city full of working-class people. Most of
them make their living in the steel mills. Lorain has fifty-six recognized ethnic groups within the city limits.

As we drove to meet Archie at one of the schools, neatly
trimmed lawns were plastered with signs. It was nearing primary
election time. Some of the names we noticed were Bulzomi, Si-
wierka, Betelski, Granada, Hritsko, Pincura, Gotis, Gradisek—and
not a whole lot of Smith-Jones-Brown types.

A visitor might get the early impression that Lorain is the kind
of city where prejudice against blacks might prevail.

"The city is not without problems," said Ruth Ann Plate, the
reading consultant for the Lorain schools. "There have been some
incidents, but having been in Boston and Pittsburgh and a
Cleveland suburb, I think we do extremely well. I live in an
upper-middle-class neighborhood, and we have whites, blacks,
Spanish—all of them living together as neighbors. We live
peacefully. This is a panorama of mixed racial groups. This truly
is a melting pot, or as we prefer to call it, a salad bowl.

"We have some homes where only Spanish is spoken in the

home—so there is a need for a lot of individualized instruction within the school system. We have to make considerable adjustments in some reading and general-instruction programs. For example, we have more than two hundred native Americans—I mean Indians—in our schools. So we have a recognized American Indian program in our schools."

Virginia Kunkle, a confessed Buckeye football fan, selected Archie for the program because of his ability to communicate with young people and because of his own academic record. Just before he began the tour of schools, Archie had been recognized by the National Collegiate Athletic Association as one of the top five scholar-athletes in the country. At Ohio State, Archie Griffin learned a whole lot more than merely football signals.

So it was not a matter of capitalizing on Archie Griffin's fame for a fleeting moment or two. In was an elaborate plan, to use the Griffin appeal to stimulate reading, then to follow up his appearances by placing a trained director in each of the 617 school districts in the state of Ohio, and in the nonpublic school areas as well, to make sure the enthusiasm didn't die out.

It was near the end of the long tour when we joined Archie. An official suggested we sit where we could see the faces of the children, and catch their expressions as they listened to their idol. The gymnasium was packed with about five hundred young people.

"There are two really fine glows about this program," she promised. "First, the glow on the faces of the children—in seeing a hero like Archie, of course, but also in listening to his message and realizing that he's so much more than just a great athlete. The second glow is finding out that the message he delivers really is taking hold. We've had hundreds of letters, not just from administrators and teachers, but also from little schoolchildren who've told of the tremendous impact Archie has had. Some of them have come from people who were very much opposed to the program at the outset—and it takes a special person to stand up and admit he was wrong. One person wrote a letter to the editor, and said he'd been really ticked off when he read that Archie was getting $125 a day—but in his letter he said, 'Whatever you're paying him, it isn't nearly enough.' That's the sort of response that is truly gratifying."

Archie Griffin had sent out written messages to the schoolchildren, in pamphlets distributed through the schools. There had been plenty of advance work, not unlike the work that precedes the arrival of an evangelist or a politician.

In some schools, before Archie's arrival, students wrote poetry and songs about Archie, or about reading, or about both.

At the Irving Elementary School in Lorain, the students had competed in an essay contest on what is important about reading. The music class at Mason School had put together a song to the tune of "You Gotta Be a Football Hero to Get Along with the Beautiful Girls."

And because these elementary school children most likely had never heard that old song, the class sang the original words:

> "*You gotta be a football hero to get along with*
> *the beautiful girls;*
> "*You gotta be a touchdown getter, if you wanna get*
> *a blonde or brunette;*
> "*The fact that you're rich and handsome won't*
> *get you anything in curls;*
> "*You gotta be a football hero to get along with*
> *the beautiful girls.*

The kids from Mason came up with this adaptation:

> "*You gotta be a reading expert to get along in*
> *the beautiful world;*
> "*For if you want your life to be a success,*
> "*You cannot do less, you must do your best;*
> "*The fact that you're rich and handsome*
> "*Will only make the ladies smirk;*
> "*But you must be a careful reader*
> *to get good and reliable work.*"

So it's no threat to Rodgers and Hammerstein.

At some schools, the entourage took Archie's Heisman Trophy along.

Margaret Lloyd, head of the Ohio Reading Improvement Effort, represented the state at many of Archie's speeches.

"You know, never once did I hear him utter one word that smacked of brashness or cockiness," she said. "At every turn, he told of the team effort, and how the other players were so outstanding that they made him appear good. He's truly one of the most humble people I've ever met."

Another thing—Archie's day generally began at 8 A.M., when he'd begin his day at one school's assembly. He'd go from there to another school, then ordinarily drive to a neighboring city. There'd be lunch at the school, then appearances at two more schools.

"Not once was he late," said Ms. Lloyd, "and not once did he ever lose his cool. He has a ton of patience, and he genuinely seemed to enjoy every minute of it.

"He seemed to revel in doing extra work. He just couldn't say 'No' to a single soul. If we had an extra few minutes, he'd insist on going to other rooms—even to kindergarten classes. He was like the Pied Piper, with young people following him all over the place."

Lorain was a classic example. Archie's lunch (he ate in the teachers' dining room) was interrupted half a dozen times—not by students, mind you, but by teachers who didn't even lie and say they wanted his autograph for a favorite nephew. It was for the teachers, and they made no bones about it.

Several teachers told me Archie had provided the motivation they'd somehow not created for the students. Said one: "You know, I just love him, even though he's made me aware of my shortcomings as a teacher—not just because of his great patience with kids, but also because he makes me realize that as a teacher I have failed to motivate my students. I simply haven't done as good a job as I should have. But because of Archie, I'm going to be a better teacher."

Some schools planned parades and had neglected to send advance notice to Archie's tour group. Not once did he complain about riding in the cold in an open car. Never did he say, "I don't feel like doing that."

"He's fantastic," said Ms. Lloyd, "just unbelievable. Frankly, people took advantage of his good nature, but he never quit smiling—and after so many days and so many schools and so many people bugging him, you could tell the smile was a genuine one."

One time, so many children lined up for autographs as Archie was trying to work in a sandwich between appearances that some of the students took charge. They asked the other students to wait outside the lunchroom until Archie had finished his meal. They even guarded the doors. When the principal of the school sought to get in for an autograph, the students stopped him. He returned after Archie had completed his lunch.

Before Archie began his tour of the Lorain schools, I asked him about the crowds crushing him:

"I guess I've always been a happy person. I can count on one hand the times I've been really mad. Once during a high school football game some kid took a cheap shot at my brother and we sort of got into a little tussle. Another time, some of the Iowa players were taking some cheap ones at me, and it upset me a little bit.

"But in football, I always figured that if someone hit me hard—and I got up quickly and had a smile on my face—it might upset the guy who did the hitting. I've been hurt a few times, but I tried never to let on.

"As for my attitude, I really can't explain how I got it except that I came from a happy home. And if you smile at somebody, it makes someone smile at you. If you go around with a frown on your face, you get the same frown in return. Sure, this tour has been tiresome at times, but if someone is nice enough to ask for my autograph, I'm gonna give it to them. I don't know—I just feel if they've taken the time to see me and ask me, they must really want it."

Today, the star athlete is more likely to brush off the autograph seeker than to stop and sign a book or a scrap of paper. One famous Hollywood personality has been quoted as saying, more than once, "I don't owe the public a thing except a good performance."

Archie has a different philosophy.

"If someone is a star, or whatever you wish to call him, the public made him a star. Without the public, no one is a star. I just hope I never change, and I really don't think I will."

The youngsters of the Irving Elementary School had weeks to prepare for Archie's visit. Some pressed letters in his hand and gave him poems they had written about him. Teachers and administrators were falling all over him as much as the students.

The crowd was lined up for autographs long before the assembly began. One teacher suggested that Archie sign his name just once and said the school could run off a whole batch of autographs on a copying machine.

"I don't think that'd be fair," said Archie. "Maybe it'd mean a little more to them to have individual autographs."

One tyke who wore his Ohio State jersey to class that day protested, "We want the real thing."

With Archie, they got it.

There were more than six hundred students gathered in the auditorium. They were from predominantly white, blue-collar environments. Many of their parents had come from Appalachia—southern Ohio and southwestern Pennsylvania and West Virginia.

They sang "America the Beautiful" to start things off, and I wondered how many folks felt like I always have—that this song is so much prettier than the one we use for our National Anthem, and speaks so much more eloquently about our nation.

Some things never change in schools—whether it's Middleport

High School in 1949 or Irving Elementary School in 1975—the piano was out of tune. There was the Pledge of Allegiance, and these kids knew the words and spoke them in loud, clear voices.

The lady who introduced Archie talked about how he was unlike some athletes, who excel on the field and fall short in the classroom. She stressed his academic achievements, his citizenship, and his willingness to spend time with young people.

Then it was Archie's turn. It took minutes for the applause to die down. I was told that at some other schools, the youngsters' enthusiasm was so great that Archie had to speak to them to get some quiet—but once he asked for it, he got it.

Once he began speaking to the students at Irving, there was absolute silence. And Archie spoke without notes. Here's what he said:

"Thank you. It's a pleasure to be here in the Irving School. I have been traveling through the city of Lorain this morning, and I find it to be a very fascinating town. I really am enjoying my travels. As a matter of fact, one of the best linemen who blocked for me during my career at Ohio State was Kurt Schumacher. You students and all the people of Lorain should be very proud of him.

"For those of you who don't know much about me, I am from Columbus, Ohio. I was born and raised there. I come from a fairly large family—six brothers and one sister, all of whom are pretty athletic. My family loves sports, but my parents taught all of us that education comes before sports. So before I went out to get my bumps and bruises, I had to first get into my books, because that's more important.

"My folks didn't have the opportunity to get college educations, but they wanted to see all of their children have that chance they didn't have. And I'm certain all your parents feel the same way.

"Right now, I'd like to share with you an experience I had when I was in junior high school in Columbus. When I was in junior high school, there was a man who had a big impact on my life. He was a teacher and my adviser for the Student Council. At that particular time, I happened to be president of the Student Council. I remember this man sitting down and talking with us during our ninth-grade year, and he told us about three things that were very important to us then, and in later life. He talked about the "three *d*'s"—and he called them desire, dedication, and determination.

"I remember he told us that if we applied these three things in our lives, we could do anything we set our minds to. He said there was nothing we couldn't achieve. And ever since that day, I have used those three *d*'s in my education and in my athletics. They've always seemed to work for me. I believe the reason Ohio State football teams are successful is because the players and the coaches know what those three things are all about. I just wanted to pass those three things on to you in the hope that you'll use them. I'm convinced they'll work for all of you like they've worked for me.

"Now, I'm sure a lot of you are wondering why a football player is here to talk to you about reading. Well, all of us need to read, and we need to read well, because it helps us in our learning. And learning makes us feel good. The more we know, the better we feel. Reading, and learning, will help us get a good job when we get out of school. I can remember that a long time ago I felt a desire to be successful, and I want every one of you to be successful, too.

"Reading is the basis for all education, and everyone can be a winner in life through reading. You can make a comparison between reading and football—it's all a learning process. I want to share a few things with you about football, and compare these things with football. First, when you play football, the coach gives you a playbook, and in that book there are plays. We use those plays and signals in our game plans throughout the season. There's lots of information that all of us need.

"When you play football, you not only compete against the other team, but also against yourself. If you're successful, you get better each and every time you step onto the field. In reading, you should read more and more, and thus get better every day. In life, all of us should be better today than we were the day before —and not quite as good as we'll be tomorrow. In football, or in anything else, you must have a positive attitude—a "Yes, I can" attitude. Sometimes you'll make mistakes. I know I've made lots of them playing football, but every time I've made a mistake, I've tried to make sure I didn't make that same mistake again.

"And when you read, many times you'll come across a word that you won't understand. The best thing to do is read and study that word, and learn its meaning—and do it over and over again, so the next time you see the word you'll know exactly what it means. The more words you know, the better you'll be able to communicate with other people, and the more about the world you'll be able to understand.

"In football, we have coaches to help us understand things and solve problems. If we have problems with a play, the coach irons out that problem—you know, he sort of helps us iron out the wrinkles, then we know what the play is all about. In school, your teachers are the coaches, and they're here to help you learn. You can't get anywhere if you don't have some direction. In order to learn, you have to have discipline. In life, no one can really discipline you like you can discipline yourself. You have to want to succeed, to sacrifice, to do whatever is necessary to get better.

"Football is a game plan, and so is life. You can't get anywhere in football without a game plan and proper execution of that plan through hard work and dedication and discipline. In football, you have to struggle to reach a worthwhile goal. Football teaches you how to win, and how to accept it when you lose, and how to cope with pressure. It's the same way in the classroom and the same way in life. You know, Coach Hayes always told us at Ohio State that you could never get anywhere if you can't take direction, learn, and discipline yourself. And he always said that people who couldn't do those things—well, they just couldn't make his teams.

"And those who can't do those things will find it hard in life. In football, you get knocked down, no matter who you are and no matter how good you might be. You just have to struggle, and get up and try to make it toward a goal.

"I was lucky enough to play a lot in my freshman year at Ohio State, and there was a lot of pressure on me. And the pressure got even greater. I remember after I won the Heisman Trophy after my junior season, wherever I'd go, people would pat me on the back and say, 'Don't worry, Archie, you'll win the Heisman Trophy again.' But the pressure was even greater my senior year, even though we had another great team—because people expected so much of all of us. But our team had discipline. Our team was willing to listen to the coaches and to learn. Our team was willing to take direction.

"Not all of us at Ohio State were fortunate enough to make the All-America team, but believe me I never could have made it, and I could never have gotten the recognition I did, without tremendous help not only from my teammates but also from my coaches. Not everyone can be an All-American football player, but you can join me and be an All-American reader. We can be on an All-American team together—I mean, really together!

"I really want you to join me on this team. If we all become good readers, we won't have to worry later in life about not understanding something. For example, we won't look at a pro football contract, or whatever kind of proposal we have in front of us, and not understand the full meaning of it. Reading is the basis for all education. Reading is the basis for understanding.

"You'll be receiving a brochure, and it has my picture and an autograph on it. In this brochure, you'll learn how you can write to me and receive the reading winner letters and All-American certificates. This brochure is entitled *Read to Win.* And that's what it's all about—winning. And don't think that because summer is coming up this program won't take place. It goes right on through the summer, and you can read books in the summertime and win awards for it. So why don't we all get together? Let's run toward the goal to make touchdowns, but this time, let's make touchdowns as better readers. Let's read to win."

More than twenty years before Archie's talk at that grade school in northern Ohio, the man to whom this book is dedicated gave me the formula for a successful speech: Have a good beginning, a good ending, and put them as close together as possible.

It always worked for him, and it had worked for Archie. He hadn't tried to tell any funny stories. He spoke without notes but without hesitation. He spoke the same way he played the game of football—with good speed, going straight ahead, following his assignment, and reaching the goal.

There wasn't a moment of uncertainty, not a single stammer. He was direct and effective. When he sat down, the applause was deafening. One of the teachers grinned and placed her forefingers in her ears to cut down on the noise. It didn't bother Archie. He'd been hearing applause for too many years, and it had become a way of life.

There was some time for questions from the audience, and one of the first questions asked Archie was, "What kind of books do you read?"

Archie's response was that he liked adventure books, sports books, and books about the Bible—"especially books about the Bible."

One young man quickly asked if a lot of the players on the Ohio State football team were Christian, and Archie said, "Yes—quite a few—and I think that's given our team special unity, a special togetherness."

One of the officials with Archie finally had to cut off the questions. A good thing, else some of the eager youngsters might have passed up their entire summer vacations just to look at this very special man and share some time with him. As Archie closed, he thanked the students for their kindness in coming to see him, and then said, "Remember, reading is to the mind what exercise is to the body."

We walked outside, and flocks of the admiring youngsters followed Archie to the parking lot, where a car was waiting to whisk him to another appearance at another school. He'd make essentially the same speech. It would have the same beautiful impact, and the youngsters would race home after school to tell their parents and sisters and brothers, "I saw Archie Griffin today."

The whole thing left Archie with a better feeling, too.

By the time his tour of the state was concluded, he had made his presentation 84 times and spoken to 50,332 students—not counting the extra stops he made, the unscheduled ones in the extra classrooms along the way.

How many lives would he change? How many young men and women would he inspire? That's a little like asking how many people Billy Graham reaches in a crusade. If there were 50,000 in the audience, aren't they all better for having heard him? If 1,000 come forward, isn't it a good thing, even if only half or a third of the conversions or rededications take? Isn't it good even if just one life is improved because of it?

"You know," said Archie, thinking back on this speech and dozens of others like it, "I wonder what'll happen to these kids. I really do. There are so many temptations these days. I'm sure a lot of them come from really good families where there's a Christian environment and where God truly is the center of the home. But I'm sure lots of them have nothing but hassles at home. I'm lucky. I've always had love and discipline in the home, and I don't believe you can really separate the two.

"Lots of times in my talks I'd talk about my home life. Even if a kid's home life isn't what it should be, I hope he can see through me that a good home life is important—and maybe that kid will realize more and more the importance of things like that. Maybe they'll be better fathers and mothers when they begin to raise their own families."

Had someone prepared his material for him for the tour?

"Well, the folks at the Board of Education knew what they wanted. They wanted a certain kind of message, and they wanted the students to be motivated. I had the basic idea to work with, but I came up with some kind of speech. Mrs. Kunkle wanted preparation and she wanted to hear what I'd say, so I gave the speech in front of her. It isn't enough just to go someplace and stand up there in front of a bunch of kids and say, 'Hi, I'm Archie Griffin. Look at me. I'm an All-American and I won the Heisman Trophy twice.' That wouldn't be very meaningful.

"You see, I had good examples when I was growing up. I had those examples right in my own home. Maybe some of these kids don't have that. I can remember some of the kids I grew up with. A kid named John was the bully of the neighborhood. He beat me up a couple of times, I guess just because he felt like it. Later on, when I was in the fifth grade, he beat up this little kid, and it really made me mad, and I told him about it. So he started on me. This time, I beat him up. He was always into trouble. I found out later he wound up in the state hospital for the criminally insane.

"Another kid in the gang on Rich Street was just about like John. His name was Dit. He stole cars and everything. Later he wound up in the penitentiary.

"I remember a guy named Andrew. He got shot robbing a filling station and went to jail. He wound up in a wheelchair. He was so bad that one time he tried to rob a dry-cleaning place while he was still in his wheelchair.

"The one thing all these guys had in common was that they had terrible home lives. We just had a different set of rules in our house, that's all. We had certain times to report in, and if we stayed out after dark, we had to be right out in front. Generally it was my mother who did the whipping. But we didn't get many whippings. I guess we just didn't get out of line very much.

"I guess my father never whipped me. He always worked so hard he wasn't home very much, but he had great big hands. All of us kinda felt if he ever hit us, it'd really hurt. That kept us in line, too. I worry that today there's hardly anyone around keeping kids in line. We seem to have forgotten all about discipline, but I don't think making a young person toe the line shows you hate him—I think it's the best kind of love."

Some weeks before, there had been a story in a major newspaper about more and more young married couples deciding not to have children, because of the turbulent social conditions and the uncertainties of the world. Maybe it was because that generation, embarking on married life amid staggering divorce statistics, had really gone without a hero.

But the youngsters all over the state of Ohio had one, and somehow Archie Griffin managed to relish the role without brashness.

"It makes me feel good, it really does," he said. "I had heroes when I was a kid, but I never dreamed anyone would look up to me. I always thought I'd try to live a pretty good life and make my parents and family proud of me, and I knew I'd someday want my children to be proud of me, but I never thought about becoming a hero to anyone. But when these kids clap for me and let out a cheer or something when I show up, it gives me a tingle. Maybe it'd sound cool if I said I'm used to it and all that, but I still feel tremendous when someone appreciates me. I hope I never do anything to make people change their minds, and I hope I never lose the good feeling I get from the good feelings of other people."

Archie jumped into a waiting car, for still another message of inspiration at still another school where little children had been anticipating his visit for weeks and weeks. He'd tell them about desire, dedication, and determination, and he'd do it looking straight into their faces. And when some tyke touched him and said, "Archie, I think you're the greatest," he'd show genuine embarrassment. And when they asked him about winning the Heisman Trophy, he'd remember that one of his teammates came from that area, too, and he'd talk about how the other members of the squad made it possible for him to grab off most of the headlines. And he'd mean every word of it, and they'd know that, too.

There had been a young man at Lorain at one of the schools, and he had hidden behind a stairwell to get the first glimpse of Archie as he came through the doors. He did not ask for an autograph, nor did he attempt to shake hands with Griffin. He was too bashful even to ask a question. But Archie spotted him right away and quickly reached out and put his arm around the young man's shoulder, asking, "How are you?"

How he was, was entranced, that's how. Archie kind of swept the boy along with him, for a few steps, then a horde of youngsters descended, and Archie was quickly swept inside an office. The boy became an instant hero with his peers because Archie had touched him and spoken to him.

Later this young man would give an interesting answer as to why he so wanted to meet Archie Griffin:

"I've never seen him play football, except on television, but he always seemed like such a great person, I just wanted to see him one time up close, that's all. I knew he'd be nice in person. I just knew it."

The little fellow was asked how he could be so certain Archie would be nice.

"I don't know, but I knew," he replied. "He's never been anything but nice, has he?"

I told him I knew of no time he'd been anything but a nice fellow. Then I asked him if he knew of anyone who perhaps didn't like Archie quite so much because he's black.

"No one I know," said the young man. "Why? What difference would that make?"

I told him it didn't, to me and obviously not to him. To some, though, it would make a difference. And I thought about a song that country artist Tom T. Hall had written and recorded, and in that song, "Old Dogs, Children, and Watermelon Wine," an old black man allowed as how those three things were all he really cared about. In the song was the line ". . . and God bless little children, while they're still too young to hate."

And I remembered a father who had responded with a cuff across the mouth when a young son first uttered the word "nigger" and the father had told him, "Son, prejudice and hatred have to be taught, and we don't teach those things in this house."

Obviously, they weren't being taught in this young man's house in Lorain, Ohio, either.

It was not too many years ago that successful and well-known football coaches at some schools in the South would call coaches up North to recommend a particular black player. Blacks have not been playing and starring at some southern schools all that long. Duffy Daugherty, when he was coaching at Michigan State, could rattle off the names of a dozen outstanding black players he recruited—with precious little effort—for the Spartans. They came to him on the recommendation of friends in the coaching fraternity. They happened to be coaching at schools not quite ready to open up their athletic programs to blacks.

It's folly to think that there are not black-white problems even today at schools both in the North and the South.

"There are always some issues that could become problems," said Woody Hayes, "and all coaches are, or should be, aware of the potential for problems. But Archie Griffin, more than any other player—black or white—who ever played at Ohio State eased every possible tension and gave our squads a unity they could never have achieved without him. He brought with him a dignity and a quiet leadership that simple excluded any possible trouble spots."

Despite the street talk that some had tried to pound into him about Hayes favoring whites, Archie said he never felt any kind of prejudice, never experienced any kind of trouble during his entire career. So it was shocking to him when some controversy arose about his job with the Department of Education, and when some Columbus residents protested when it was suggested the city name a street for him.

Was it possible that the same folks who had plastered their automobiles with "Thank You, Mrs. Griffin" stickers now had wrung every ounce of football out of this young man and were the same ones leading the chorus of protestors?

"I never asked anyone to name anything after me," said Archie, more baffled than angry over the issue. "The Bible tells us we shouldn't go around seeking credit for various things but that we should walk humbly, and that's what I've tried to do. When someone asked me what I thought about the idea, I told them it didn't matter. I didn't want it to sound like I wasn't honored just by the idea, but I just didn't want anything connected with me to start any fuss."

And the fuss over his so-called high-paying job, going around meeting and talking with elementary school students?

"I guess I'd have quit the whole thing and walked away from it, but down deep in my heart I figured I might be able to do some good with those kids. I didn't talk to them just about reading, you know. I talked about my family life and my belief in God and the importance of doing your best no matter what you're doing. And wherever I went, I really got good vibrations from the kids. I think they could relate to me. They seemed to pay attention to what I had to say. I don't want it to sound cocky, but I really believe I did some good. The criticism bothered me, but it's a little like someone belittling you before a big game, or putting you down and saying you don't have very much ability or saying they're going to throw up a defense that's sure to stop you. Things like that just make you play a little harder, and give a little extra, I think. So I made sure when I went on that tour and talked with all those kids, I put a little extra effort into it."

The one thing, the single criticism that bothered Archie more than anything else, and lingers with him to this day, is the post-Rose Bowl criticism directed at his teammate, Cornelius Greene.

"I still ache when I think about that," Archie said. "It has to be the most unfair criticism in the world. Here's a guy who played his heart out his entire career and they get all over him because he had one bad game. We all had a bad game in that Rose Bowl. But you look it up—in the 1974 Rose Bowl he was voted the Most Valuable Player [we looked it up, and Greene was], and in the '74 season he gained more yards than I did. You look that up and see if I'm not right [Archie's right; Greene gained 1,781 on 842 yards rushing and 939 yards passing, while Archie had 1,695, all on the ground], and then you check out his sophomore year. He gained over a thousand yards as a sophomore [1,063, to be exact], and without him we wouldn't have gotten to the Rose Bowl that last year.

"No one said anything about his flashy style as long as we kept winning. No one criticized Corny for anything. We all kidded him about his fancy clothes, but that's his way. He's just a flashy guy. But no one said anything bad about him. No one accused him of messing around with dope or anything like that. But just for one defeat, there are people who would wreck his entire life, and it's just not fair."

During the entire outpouring, Archie never once raised his voice, yet for him it was a tirade. It seemed he was more hurt than the one accused of throwing the game.

Cornelius Greene has tried to forget about it but confesses it's not easy to do.

"But I honestly don't think it bothered me as much as it did Griff," he ventured. "Maybe it's the difference in our personalities, but it just about broke Archie's heart. I've tried to shake it off, and figure it's the work of a few evil people who lost some money on the game and who had to have someone to lash out against. But it crushed Archie even to think there are people around who think like that."

The Rose Bowl loss to UCLA marred an otherwise perfect season for the Buckeyes. It was something they had not experienced since 1968. There had been the unexplainable loss to Michigan in the final game of 1969, the Rose Bowl defeat to Stanford after the 1970 campaign, and the 10–10 with Michigan in the 1973 windup. And perhaps only the diehard loyalists can understand Woody Hayes' frustration after losing to a team his Buckeyes had beaten soundly earlier in the year. This was, after all, the finale to his silver anniversary coaching season at the school. It was the final game for the player he had described as the best he'd ever seen or coached. It cost his team the national championship and perhaps snatched the Coach of the Year honors away from him.

Was it then excusable that he slammed the door in the face of newsmen he had charmed for so long, and said not a word? Was it pardonable that he did not give warm congratulations to Dick Vermeil, who had done a superior job of getting his UCLA team prepared to knock off the best college football team in the land? Was it understandable that even after the long return trip home, the man would maintain a stony silence in front of the loyalists who considered him more messiah than mentor?

Being a sore loser is not even a misdemeanor for Woody Hayes. And nothing said or done since would indicate that if he had it to do all over again, the old coach would behave any differently. Five times before that in his career, a single football game had separated his teams from unsullied records, but this, surely, was the most crushing setback of all. There simply were too many ingredients that went into making this what could have been the best season of all time for him.

"Every once in a while I still think back to that game," said Archie, "but it's not going to be a monkey that's gonna stay on my back for the rest of my life. But I have to believe that Coach Hayes just will never ever let it get out of his mind. I haven't talked with him about it. It's just not something you would bring up. But I think I know how much it meant to him and how much it hurt him. It's not that he wants to win any more than I do, it's rather a case of him being around on this earth a whole lot longer and he had so much more built into this one game. But I still wish he would have said something gracious after the game—just anything, instead of saying nothing. But I guess if he had behaved any differently, it wouldn't have been Coach Hayes."

Perhaps Woody Hayes will never permit himself to forget that game, but for the record he tells interviewers, "Hell, that game's over and done with. We've had lots of games since then, and every one is a different challenge." But those close to him swear it's the one game that meant more than all the rest.

For Cornelius, he'll remember the devastating loss to UCLA more than any of the thirty-five games he started for the Ohio State Buckeyes.

"At first, I didn't know anything about it," he said. "I had gone out to Honolulu to play in the Hula Bowl. Things were so terrible after the game I didn't want to see anybody and I didn't want to talk to anybody. The players didn't even go around the locker room trying to console each other. It was miserable. Archie finally came out to Hawaii, and I guess maybe a couple of times he tried to bring the subject up—to tell me what was going on back in Columbus and what some folks were saying. But when we finally got back to Columbus, he got it all out into the open. I'm sure he felt worse about it than I did. But I couldn't believe it myself.

"Archie and I are different types of cats. I mean, he grew up with his parents, and I grew up with my aunt and uncle. I know things were pretty tough for Archie when he was growing up because there wasn't much money. My aunt and uncle did everything for me and made sure I always had nice things and nice clothes. They're the ones who bought me my car while I was in college. I suppose Archie mentioned that, didn't he, and how upset Coach Hayes was? Anyway, Archie's conservative, where on the other hand I've always been very flashy.

"When we heard all the chatter that I had thrown the game, that I had bet on UCLA and that I had gotten forty or fifty thousand dollars to dump the game. Well, let's put it this way: I wasn't as terribly shocked about it as Archie. Archie's awfully innocent and sometimes a little naïve. He really believes basically that all people are good and that no one wants to do bad things or even think them. I know differently. I know some people are just evil and will do or say anything to justify their own misery. While I was tremendously upset by those rumors, I can't say I was totally shocked.

"When I heard a story going around that someone was planning to plant dope in my apartment, then call the police, I went straight to Coach Hayes and told him about it. I wanted someone else to know about it in case it actually happened. The worst part of it all is that stories like that circulated among some kids. Now, kids are pretty impressionable, you know, even in today's world. And you run around and tell kids some wild story about betting and dope and all that, and you point out to them that we lost to a team we had pretty well handled earlier in the season—well, you just can't wipe out the damage something like that can do. The most frustrating part of it all is that you can't defend against it. What are you going to do, run around and knock on every door in town and say, 'Hey, I'm Corny Greene and I'm here to tell you that I did my best in the Rose Bowl and I really didn't throw the game'? There's no way. You just gotta take it, that's all."

It's a good thing no one actually dared confront Cornelius Greene and directly accuse him of such a deed. It would have put his faith to a strenuous test.

"I know I'm a Christian and I know what the Word says, but I'd have had a terrible time turning the other cheek. I know in my heart I would have wanted to lash back. But no one ever had the courage to say anything to my face. It was all behind my back."

A year and a half later, where does that awful experience leave Cornelius Greene? What has it done to him, to his faith in people?

"I suppose the thing that bothered me most, even before the Rose Bowl defeat, was learning that there are some people you can never satisfy. There are some people you can't change, some you can't reason with. Some people just don't have good sense or good morals either, for that matter. They've been spoiled here. I mean, a one-loss season just isn't good enough for these folks. We were 11–0 going into the Rose Bowl, but that one loss set 'em off. They forgot the eleven victories. Everything was wiped out in their minds because of one football game.

"They go around chanting, 'We're No. 1,' and they paste

9A. *Left,* If anyone thought Archie Griffin's 239-yard rushing output against North Carolina in his freshman year was a fluke, he proved otherwise later that same year. He gained even more yardage against Illinois and got loose for a long gainer on this quick-opener. 10. *Right,* Going. . . .

11. Going. . . .

12. *Top,* Kerplop! Archie Griffin says the hardest hitting always came in the Michigan games, and in this sequence of pictures by Barry Edmonds, chief photographer for the Flint *Journal,* Archie finds himself overcome by unfriendly people. This happened in the 1975 Ohio State-Michigan game at Ann Arbor. 13. *Middle,* This was a typical scene in an Ohio State-Michigan game. Archie said every time he looked up, there'd be a Michigan player ready to hit him. This action is from the 1973 game, and Michigan's Dave Brown is taking aim on Archie. 14. *Bottom,* Archie learned early there's nothing quite like the Michigan game. The first time he played against the archrival Wolverines, his Ohio State team got a big break when Michigan fumbled away the football at Ohio State's one-yard line.

15. *Above left,* The Gophers of Minnesota never could stop Archie Griffin, and here he breaks a tackle en route to a long gainer in the 1973 game. 16. *Above right,* It was a reflective—and tired Archie Griffin who went to the sidelines after another scintillating performance, against Illinois in 1974. 17. *Below,* The chant was "We're No. 1" after a resounding Ohio State victory over Illinois in early November 1974, and Archie Griffin—on the shoulders of his teammates—was leading the cheering.

18. *Above left,* It was bye-bye Mustangs in 1974 as Archie Griffin got loose for a touchdown in a game against Southern Methodist. 19. *Above right,* Pete Johnson got a record number of touchdowns for Ohio State, but much of the time Pete (No. 33) was moving people out of the way for Archie Griffin, as he did here in the Wisconsin game in 1975. 20. *Right,* That's not a look of anger, rather of contentment on the face of Woody Hayes. The Ohio State coach had just seen his team claw back from a 14–7 deficit to defeat Michigan, 21–14, in the final moments of the 1975 game. Woody called this Ohio State's best come-from-behind achievement.

stickers all over their cars and everywhere else. Spirit is great and it's necessary, but it's just that some people carry it too far. I know winning is important, and no one loves it more than I do. I think I'm a winner. I'm accustomed to winning. I never enjoyed losing anything in my life. We had four straight Big Ten championships and lost only five games in four years, but for some, it wasn't enough. I don't know, maybe it would have satisfied them if we had gone out and jumped into the Pacific Ocean and drowned ourselves. But I didn't think anyone had to come back to Columbus with his tail between his legs. Basically, I'd like to think that college football is still a game. And it's being played by kids, really. It's supposed to be fun, but the fans put too much pressure on the young men who play the game."

Cornelius Greene was just a teen-ager when he won the starting quarterback job at Ohio State. Greg Hare had been the regular the year before but pulled a hamstring muscle two weeks before the season opener against Minnesota. So the job, apparently for the time being, fell to a nineteen-year-old who had been a high school All-American just two years before, at Dunbar High School in Washington, D.C. Coach Hayes had rarely trusted his offense to such an inexperienced hand, but Greene had impressed even the crusty old mentor in the spring game when he ran for 116 yards and passed for 137 more (a season's output for most Ohio State teams) and showed good leadership in the huddle. Greene brought leadership with him to Ohio State, having been elected captain of his football, basketball, and baseball teams in high school.

By the time he was thrust into a starter's role, he and Archie Griffin were the best of friends. The friendship had begun warily. Their first meeting was during a practice session shortly after they had arrived on campus as freshmen.

"We were running some 40-yard sprints one day and I saw this muscular little guy running like the dickens. He did a 4.5 and I turned to Woodrow Roach, who was from Washington, and said, 'Hey, they're not kidding about having fast guards here.' I really thought he was a lineman. In high school, we had guards who were about 180 and he had these muscles, and he waddled so, that he just looked like a guard to me. Then when someone told me that was Archie Griffin, I flipped. I had heard of him because he and I were named to the same high school All-America team.

"The same coach, Rudy Hubbard, recruited both of us, but he never mentioned Archie to me. I guess after I signed to go to Ohio State, Rudy mentioned that Archie Griffin would be going there. But just because the two of us had been picked on the high school All-America team didn't mean a whole lot. It meant a lot when we were picked, but when you get on the field at a big school you can put all those newspaper clippings and trophies behind you. You have to prove yourself all over again."

A friendship involving Archie, Corny, and Woody Roach developed rapidly. Archie, the Columbus native, showed the out-of-staters around. More than that, the Griffins practically adopted Cornelius Greene.

"My folks appreciated that and I know I did," said Greene. "Right away, it was like having another family at school. I was from a family of eight and I was raised by my aunt and uncle, so it was like being raised as an only child. But I was raised in what you might call a hard ghetto area, and a lot of the kids I knew when I was growing up around Washington are, well, sort of strung out now, you might say. But still, I had a good family situation. My folks were separated, so my father's sister and her husband took me in. They didn't have any kids of their own. My father lived with us, too. And we've always had a close family relationship, all my brothers and sisters, even though I didn't actually live with them. So when I got to be good friends with Archie, the best thing of all was being around his family. They're such great people, it's hard to imagine a family being that closely knit. They're really together."

Archie Griffin was instrumental in persuading Cornelius Greene to publicly proclaim his faith in Jesus Christ.

"I learned from him," said Greene. "He's just the kind of

human being every man can learn from. I mean, he'd always be doing the right thing. Some of us goofed off once in a while. Nothing too serious, mind you. But we'd cut classes and so on, and Archie would come in and get on us about it. He never did it in a mean way. In fact, he always smiled. It seems he's always smiling, even when someone is trying to knock his head off. But he'd come into the room and admonish us a little bit. And finally it started to soak in that 'Hey, this guy is right and the rest of us are wrong.' I guess that's what started me thinking and got me on the right track.

I used to say it wasn't a matter of being non-Christian, but I guess if you're not a devoted, full-time active Christian, then you're really not a Christian at all. I didn't think I was all that bad, but when I looked at Archie and saw the goodness in him, plus the fun he was having out of life by just being good, I really saw all the things I was missing.

"My folks were believers and all that, but I wasn't forced to go to church, so I wasn't what you'd call active. I didn't have a real church life, so to speak. But I got to Ohio State and looked around, especially at Archie, and I saw what was missing in my life. It's almost amazing to see someone of that stature, really wanting to go through life as straight as that. It's pretty easy to give in to temptation when you have so much ability and you get so much attention, but Archie never wavered. He's a strong believer, so strong that he makes others around him believe.

"I guess I was baptized, or christened, as a child. But I had no real experience with a Christian baptism. And I wasn't getting the real fruits, the real blessings that come with being a Christian. I kept thinking that I was doing all right, just because I had been a star athlete in an area where there was a lot of trouble and temptation. I guess I thought just because I had turned away from those temptations, I was home free. But I wasn't. I was just going through the motions, until I got in with Archie. We spent our freshman year together, and I started going to church with him. And I had spent some time with Rex Kern (former Ohio State quarterback and active Christian layman) and had talked with him about giving my life to Christ. But the night I actually made my decision to go all the way, Archie and I were in our room together. I know he was as happy about it as I was."

Once he made his commitment, Cornelius Greene found more temptation staring him in the face.

"I don't know what I expected. I guess I thought most of my problems would be behind me. But I found that more temptations come about once you make that decision for Jesus. Then I started searching the Word of God and I discovered that the Christian is supposed to have more problems than the nonbeliever. The Bible said the believer will be persecuted and all that and that people will punish him and forsake him. And I believe that. The Devil really works on the Christian, and maybe he works doubly hard on the baby Christian. I believe the Devil would rather win back a Christian than anything else. You know, he's already got the nonbeliever on his side, so it's a real bonus if he can persuade a Christian to cast Jesus aside.

"I don't know what I'd have done when the Rose Bowl criticism came if I hadn't had the Lord on my side. I don't think I could have taken it. But because of my belief, I was able to look everyone straight in the eye and face the fact that I had a bad game, our line had a bad game, and really, our whole team had a bad game. There's no great secret about why we lost. You can cut it up any way you like, but it boils down to the fact that UCLA played better football than we did. Maybe some of the experts enjoyed dissecting the game from start to finish and coming up with fancy answers, but there was nothing to figure out at all.

"Don't misunderstand what I'm about to say, now, but if athletes took defeats as hard as some fans do, they'd never be able to get their act together to play the next game. Athletes hate to lose, and I don't want anyone ever to think I didn't hurt when my team lost. But you have to be mentally tough and put defeats behind you, or you'll wind up playing last week's defeat for several weeks. And that's contagious. This is all part of the mental disci-

pline of football. And I can equate that to Christianity, too. If
you let last week's defeats get hold of you and tear you apart,
you're no good for anything that may confront you today. You
have to be mentally tough to put sin, and setbacks, behind you.
They're supposed to make you stronger, not weaker."

But doesn't Corny's old coach let those things stick in his craw?

"I'm sure certain defeats have bothered him for a long time,
but I'll say this for the man: Never in front of the players did he
dwell on yesterdays. I know lots of folks criticize him for lots of
things, but I feel the same way about him today as I did when I
was playing for him, and that's a good feeling. He sticks by his beliefs, and he never changes. He's a lot like Archie in that respect.
They're both very disciplined people. If they have a conviction,
they stick with it. They're the same, every day. People like that
have a tremendous amount of influence on other people. They're
leaders. I guarantee you, Archie Griffin will have great impact for
good for a lot of years, because he's never gonna change. He's always gonna be good. He isn't capable of being anything else."

Corny Greene isn't certain there'll ever be another Archie
Griffin.

"Someone may break all his records. Tony Dorsett of Pittsburgh had more career yardage, and I'm not taking anything away
from what he has done. But to say that there'd be someone come
along who's as spectacular on and off the field, no way, man. All
of us have certain things we strive for, certain goals we set for ourselves. And in some respects, I believe all of us have heroes, or we
should have, anyway. And maybe we imitate someone else. But I
don't think Archie Griffin had to imitate anyone. He's just being
himself, all the time. I know for a long time it was tough for me
to believe that any person could be that good—I mean, that super
straight with everyone, all the time—but he convinced me. He's a
tremendous Christian. I think Archie is what being a Christian is
all about. He's a one-of-a-kind athlete, and a one-of-a-kind human
being."

Archie Griffin would seem to have it all—respect from his peers, the admiration of children, great ability, a solid home life, a promising future, and honors galore—but it is true that it is lonelier at the top.

"You can't believe the pressure on him," said Greene. "It's easy to sit down and list the demands on his time, the requests he's had, and the things people want him to do. But to see how he operates amid all this confusion is amazing. I know I couldn't have done it and kept smiling like Archie has. Nothing ever seems to bother him, but I know some things have. He was upset about the Rose Bowl thing, sure, and he was upset when some folks criticized him for that job he had going around talking to schoolkids.

"Just because he's all the time smiling don't think he isn't affected by criticism. I remember when we were in school, someone would make some remark about him and they'd say Archie probably has a big ego and probably thinks he's hot stuff. Archie'd say to me, 'Why would someone say something like that when they don't even know me?' I know Archie better than most folks do, and I know things get to him."

The election of Pitt's Tony Dorsett as the 1976 Heisman Trophy winner left Archie Griffin the least surprised person in the world, save Dorsett himself. It was Dorsett who had publicly said he should have won it his junior year, when he finished fourth behind Archie, Chuck Muncie of California, and Ricky Bell of Southern California.

Voting for the Heisman is done in five sections, and Griffin won in the East, with Dorsett second. In fact, Griffin won in four of the five sectors, and was beaten by Muncie in the West. It was a runaway vote, where some had predicted it would be close. Archie got 454 first-place votes to 145 for the next man. Archie also got more second- and third-place votes than any other nominee, and his 1,800 total points more than doubled Muncie's total. In all, 888 electors took part.

Four others had won the Heisman Trophy in their junior years. Doc Blanchard of Army won it in 1945 but finished fourth the following year when his teammate, Glenn Davis, won the coveted prize. Doak Walker of Southern Methodist captured the laurel in 1948, but Leon Hart of Notre Dame won it the next year while Walker, who later would be Hart's teammate with the Detroit Lions, wound up third. Vic Janowicz of Ohio State won it as a junior in 1950, but injuries kept him out of the running the next season. Roger Staubach of Navy took the Heisman in 1963 but failed to place in the balloting in 1964.

More and more in recent years, columnists and broadcasters have taken to strong criticism of the Heisman voting. In addition to Warner Wolf's nationwide broadside, one syndicated columnist said Archie inherited the award instead of winning it. He agreed with Wolf that voters looked more to his four-year career than to his performance during a single season. He hauled out statistics that showed Muncie and Bell gained more yards and that another Bell, Gordon, of archrival Michigan, outgained Archie over the course of the season and outplayed him in the head-to-head confrontation in the final game of the season.

"They should call it the Hearsay Trophy," wrote columnist Steve Bisheff of Copley News Service. "You know, like 'What do you hear about this guy?' Everyone, of course, had heard all about Griffin. He's been a great little back for Ohio State. Consistent, durable, tough. He's had a marvelous career, probably as fine a four years as any amateur runner in history. But the Heisman is supposed to be based on *one* year, not four. It's an award that should go to the best player of 1975. And sorry, Archie, but on straight, objective comparisons, you don't even finish in the money this fall."

He wrote further that the voting looks more and more like a political election every year. "Candidates come and go," he said, "but the real winners are hammered out in smoke-filled rooms before the season ever begins. . . . Archie's a fine player and they say he's a super kid. But, somehow, when it comes to an honor as important as this, you prefer to see somebody go out and earn that second Heisman instead of merely inheriting it."

Archie has never met that writer. If he did, he said, he'd be gracious and kind and would never bring up that provocative and critical article.

"Why should I?" asked Archie. "He's entitled to his opinion, just like Tony Dorsett is entitled to his and like everyone is entitled. But I'm not giving the trophy back, no matter what anybody says, writes, or thinks."

Archie spoke with Dorsett over a telephone hookup for a radio station in Pittsburgh a couple of weeks before last year's Heisman voting was made public.

"I didn't bring up the things he had said. He's allowed to think those things and to say them. It's a free country. I congratulated him on winning, even though they hadn't made the announcement yet. It was pretty obvious he would win it, and I know how good it made him feel. From what I've seen, he's a tremendous runner and he'll do well in the pros. I know some people say he's not really a humble person, but I've been around him and he's been all right with me, and that's how I judge a person."

There were widespread reports that Dorsett and some cronies misbehaved on the trip to the Hula Bowl, that they zipped around in a limousine and made a habit of closing the bars each night and that on game day, Dorsett claimed he was too ill to participate in the game.

"I read something about that but I don't know what actually happened. The one thing Tony will have to understand is that he's under a microscope and whatever he does, people are gonna know about it. Maybe the reports were exaggerated. I hope so. I don't care how much talent a person has, he can wreck it all if he doesn't take care of it and if he gets his head out of place. You can't be too big. Any game in the world, whether it's football or something else, can survive without the biggest stars. And if you abuse your body, you can squander your future.

"When I make talks to young people, I try to impress upon them the importance of being disciplined in every way. Those 'three d's' I learned in junior high school are important, I think, and they're not just for kids. No matter how old we get, we still need discipline, we still need dedication, and we still need determination. You can't be physically strong and mentally tough without those things. I'm one of the lucky ones because I really learned those things early in life. The Lord blessed me with some ability, but I could throw it all away if I didn't take care of it. Whatever I have is just a loan from Jesus Christ, and it could be taken away from me unless I protect it. They're gifts, and I've always felt a person has to guard them like precious gifts, or you might wake up some day and they'll be gone.

"One of the things that really impressed me in my first year with the Bengals was seeing Coy Bacon and Bob Brown and watching the way they perform. I mean, they're quite a bit older than I am, and they're both at the age when their careers could be over and done with. But they're like kids in some ways, I mean as far as enthusiasm is concerned. They worked as hard as anyone on the team, and they bear down all the time. And when the season was over, they weren't sick and tired of football. They still were rarin' to go, and when we missed the playoffs, they were really disappointed, but right away they started talking about next year. Lots of guys in that situation would have talked about quitting, but all these guys could think about was coming back next year with a better team, and being good enough not to miss the playoffs by just a whisker. I really respect them both."

Most fans figure the truly great athlete suffers fewer setbacks and disappointments than the run-of-the-mill performer. Experts say that's not so, because the remarkable athlete sets higher standards of excellence for himself and expects more of himself.

One of the most respected and revered coaches of all time was the late Vince Lombardi, who listed his priorities as (1) God, (2) family, and (3) the Green Bay Packers. He once said that the borderline or marginal player neither suffers much nor enjoys much because "he's just glad to be there." But the star is frustrated by anything short of an outstanding performance. He'll agonize a little more over a defeat. Another thing: The star is more apt to play over pain and endure more stress.

"I've seen that over and over," Archie commented. "From the time I first started playing sports, I've seen that same thing repeated a hundred times. But very few people really become stars without great character. I'm convinced that in tight situations, whether it's in sports or in something else in life like business or warfare or whatever, the people who really come through for you are those who have the extra something down deep inside them. To me, that's character."

When he was eight and nine years old, "they" said Archie Griffin was too small to play football with the twelve- and thirteen-year-olds. When he went to Ohio State, "they" said he was too small to play at such a big school and that he'd get lost in the shuffle. When he was drafted by the Cincinnati Bengals, "they" said Archie Griffin was too small to make it in the National Football League. But "they" don't know how to measure character, perhaps because they have too little of it themselves. And "they" are the ones who are content to be spectators in the game of life. "They" are the critics who stand on the sidelines and pontificate while others go out and do battle, and "they" have to be content with vicarious thrills and never really understand the thrill of victory and the agony of defeat. "They" would be better off if "they" spent more time around the Griffin family.

# 3

## *A House Built upon a Rock*

The Griffins of Columbus, Ohio, are more than a family, more than a clan. They are an alliance held strongly together by love and mutual respect. They are an unusual breed, these people, and they have wound themselves around each other's hearts in such a way as to create an atmosphere that can be felt and affection that can be seen.

The Griffins just may have the best family life in America. Theirs is not a complex formula. Actually it's quite simple: Work hard, play whenever you can, love without ceasing, and respect everyone.

There are ten of them—Jim, Margaret, seven boys, and one girl. They will work while you and I are sleeping, create opportunities out of what others might consider incurable problems, and never, ever scream about misfortune. While the deterioration of American family life may be a national ailment, it has never hit the Griffin household. While parents and children complain about the inability to communicate with each other, the lines of communication have always been wide open at the Griffin home.

And while American Presidents for the past quarter century have been so concerned about the softness of our youth that they've created councils on physical fitness, the Griffins will beat you at any game you pick. They might even give you a head start.

They are a houseful of Jack Armstrongs but with an ever-so-gentle spirit coursing through the mainstream of their existence. They are old-fashioned, these folks, with an abundance of love for things like home, God, the flag, and apple pie.

Papa Griffin never plays cards with the boys, has never owned a set of golf clubs, and never found the time to join any social group. Mama Griffin acknowledges she'd rather he didn't work so hard so they could do more things together, but she always has understood his unique drive and his willingness, almost compulsion, to totally sacrifice himself for the overall good of his children. Margaret Monroe Griffin busies herself taking care of the remaining youngsters at home and the four married brothers who stop in regularly. The Griffin boys make a habit of not moving very far away from the family nest. Mrs. Griffin's load is a bit lighter these days, so she's become involved with a program to improve the school system, she's been active in the March of Dimes campaign, and she's chairwoman of a recruiting drive for the Young Women's Christian Association. Of course, she's always been active in school affairs and the PTA.

While the young men in the family are more gregarious, surely because of their involvement in sports, neither parent is mousy or submissive. The leadership they exert may be the quiet type, but it is leadership nonetheless. And you should not ask either Griffin parent a direct question unless you are prepared for a completely honest answer. Neither has mastered the art of lying.

Life in the coal fields around Logan, West Virginia, was not particularly kind either to the Griffins or the Monroes. The menfolk invariably worked in the mines. There were no unions then, and the hours were long and the pay short. The work was backbreaking, and the time to play was nonexistent. Merle Travis wrote a song about life in the coal mines of eastern Kentucky but the meaning was the same in West Virginia: "Sixteen tons and what do you get? Another day older and deeper in debt."

James Griffin made up his mind while still a teen-ager that he wanted no part of coal mining. He also determined then that if he ever had children, they'd have enough education to escape the drudgery of the deep mines. For years, many of the memories Jim Griffin had of his early years were unpleasant ones, but things are better for him now, and he's careful when he talks about his own late father.

"I think whatever I am today and whatever has happened to my family, you have to give a lot of credit to my father," he explained. "A lot of people thought my daddy was mean, and a lot of people didn't understand him. I guess I didn't understand him for a long time. I always wanted to be different than him in some ways, but I wanted to be like him in some ways, too. I wanted to go to college, but my daddy didn't think we could make it, so I didn't go. He just said there wasn't enough money to send me to college. I guess I would have gone to Bluefield State, and I always thought I'd like to be a lawyer. Maybe I would have gone anyway if I had realized you could go to school and work your way through. But I didn't know that then.

"My daddy believed that everything you did wrong, you had to have a whipping for it. I never did believe in that and still don't. He was an honest man, though. He always said he never lied to anybody and he wouldn't take it if a man lied to him. He stood up for what he believed in. He was a pretty tough man, I guess you'd say, and like I said, I guess a lot of people down there around Logan thought he had a mean streak in him."

His name was Archie Mason Griffin. It was not uncommon for him to leave the house at five in the morning for the mine and work well past midnight. Jim was the fourth of six children, but only three of them survived childhood.

"My mother died in childbirth when I was four. There were four of us left then, but my older brother died a few years later when he was just twelve. He came down with typhoid fever and died. Archie, Jr., Samuel, and Raymond all died when they were just little, and my sister Marguerite died a couple of years ago.

Out of six of us kids, there's just two left now, my sister Catherine
and I. She still lives in Logan."

Like most of us, Jim Griffin thought his father was a little too
tough, too strict at times, and perhaps almost unreasonable.

"But the older I get the more I appreciate him. We differed on
a lot of things. He didn't think I could do certain things, and I'd
always be trying to show him that I could. If he would be alive
today and he'd see me going out and buying a new car, he
wouldn't like it. He'd tell me I really didn't need it. When you
talk about someone ruling with an iron hand, I guess that's what
he did. But he thought in his heart he was right, so I can't fault
him for that."

Those were the most difficult days. They were the late twenties,
and the Depression was setting in for a long siege. And Jim
Griffin tries awfully hard not to remember the hard times. He
remembered everything about those days, though, when it came
to the care and feeding of his own flock.

No one questioned his father's authority. He made all the decisions. There was no consultation and no bargaining, and once his
decision was handed down, there was no appeal.

"I made up my mind when I had my kids, we'd talk things over.
I've always tried to listen to them. I may make the decisions, but
I always try to listen to everyone's side of things. And I've never
been ashamed to admit when I've been wrong. Everybody has
different things they live by, and I just live a different way than
my daddy did. He wasn't afraid to fight, but I've never cared
much about it. He had a saying that he'd never call anybody a liar
unless he was looking for a fight, and if anyone called him a liar,
then that person must be looking for a fight himself. And he'd
fight. Oh, yes, he'd fight, all right. I guess maybe some folks were
kinda scared of him, too. But he was pretty good about going to
church and things like that, and nobody could beat him provid-
ing. He saw to it that you had all that you needed.

"He made us kids go to church, too. Maybe that's why I don't
go today, because I was pushed so hard. Now, I believe and all

that. But I just don't go to church. I will, though, when I make up my mind to go. I just have to get everything straightened out in my own mind, then I'll go. I don't wanna be a hypocrite about it. I wanna make sure that everything is all right in my own heart, because if you're not all right with God, then you're all wrong with him."

It was the Griffin strength, the Griffin regard for right and distaste for wrong that brought about the union of James Griffin and Margaret Monroe. She was a shy ninth-grader, and she had gone to a dance in Logan, West Virginia.

Margaret Griffin remembers the incident as if it happened a fortnight ago:

"This boy tried to take advantage of me, and I hollered for help. Jim came to my rescue. He grabbed this other boy and told him what he'd do if he didn't leave me alone. From that day on we started going together, and we've been together ever since. That's more than thirty-five years ago, and I guess I'd have to say he hasn't changed much in all that time."

They would have gotten married when she was but fifteen years old, but her father, John Daniel Monroe, would have none of that.

"He liked Jim. He thought he was a nice person, but I guess he thought I was a little too young. So we got married when I was sixteen and Jim was nineteen. I was still in high school. He went right into the service, and I finished high school after we got married."

When Jim came back from the service, his father gave him a piece of ground, and the newlyweds built their own house. He had been in the service, then worked in the shipyards of Norfolk, Virginia, before coming back home. The old man was dead set against his son going into the mines, so Jim Griffin got a job working for the mining company, but on a coal tipple. But in 1948, there was a massive layoff, and the only way for him to keep a job was to go into the ground and mine the coal. That was the year their first son, James, was born. Two years later, there was a second son, Lawrence. Daryle came along two years later, but by this time Jim had decided he'd had enough of the coal mines and he set out for Columbus, Ohio.

That's where Archie was born. The folks decided to give him the name of Jim's father, Archie Mason Griffin, when he came into the world on August 21, 1954. Raymond, beginning his senior year at Ohio State and a candidate for All-America honors as a defensive back, was born in June of 1956. Duncan, who should be in the starting defensive secondary with the Buckeyes in the 1977 season, was born in November 1957. Keith's the one all the Griffins say has more potential than all the rest, and he'll be a sophomore at Eastmoor High this fall. The only girl in the family is Crystal and she was born in 1965.

"Being the only girl, I guess you'd have to say she's a tiny bit spoiled," says her mother. "She pretty well gets whatever she wants, especially from her father."

The Griffins make certain no one gets too spoiled.

"I know my parents like all of us to be confident," says Archie, "but there's a big difference between being confident of your ability and being cocky about it. If anybody ever got out of line, we'd have a little family talk about it."

Archie already has had some conversations with Keith.

Just last season, in junior high school football, Keith gained 893 yards and averaged more than 10 yards a carry. He scored 13 touchdowns running with the football and caught 3 touchdown passes.

"He acts more like Raymond than the rest of us. Raymond is really confident of his ability, and so is Keith. Keith will challenge anybody at anything. We have to sit on him a little bit. I told him to be careful about talking too much, but he said, 'What's wrong, if I can do it?' So I just told him that no matter how good anybody is, there'll be disappointments, no matter what. But he takes coaching well, and he's well disciplined. Daddy would make sure of that. No question about that."

Papa Griffin: "Keith has a lot of ability, and he does have

confidence. I like all our boys to have confidence. But I don't think he's too cocky. I know when we were watching the Hula Bowl on television last January, he said, 'I'm gonna be the first Griffin to play in the Hula Bowl.' Now, that sounds pretty cocky, maybe, but a minute or two later he was telling me he had to really work hard this coming fall to be sure and make the high school team. You see, all our boys have competed pretty hard against each other. All of them made their high school teams the first try, so Keith has to live up to what the others have done."

What the others have done is considerable.

The oldest brother, Jim, went to Muskingum of Ohio, starred at halfback on offense, and played cornerback on defense. Larry went to Louisville and excelled at fullback. Daryle went to Kent State and had an outstanding career as a defensive halfback. Archie, Raymond, and Duncan went to Ohio State, and it's assumed by everyone that once Keith finishes what figures to be a tremendous high school career, he'll follow in the footsteps of Archie, Raymond, and Duncan.

"It's a little early to talk about it," said Archie, "but still, people do talk about it. Keith hasn't said anything, but I imagine he'd like to go to Ohio State. I know he'll go to college somewhere, because that's just the way it is in our family."

All the Griffin boys except Jim got full scholarships because of their athletic skills. Jim would have, except that Muskingum gave only half scholarships for sports.

The basement of the Griffin home on the east side of Columbus is literally filled to overflowing with trophies the Griffin men have won. Talk too much about Archie's accomplishments, and the patriarch will show you scads of awards and plaques the others have won. There are no favorites in the house, and the awards are considered family possessions.

"I have a few of my trophies and one of the Heisman trophies, but my mom and daddy just started collecting them and putting them up from the time we were in grade school. That's just where they belong, and we never think about it. If anybody wants to see them, that's where they are. People have asked me why I include my family in everything. Well, it's because I owe everything to them. They've given me every little bit they had. They've done the same for all the kids. They took time out to watch me from the time I was nine years old, even when I didn't get to play very much. If I got in just for the last two minutes, I could depend on them being there."

When Archie was nine, he didn't get to play too much for the Maryland AC team—because the other players ranged in age from twelve to fifteen.

"I was a fat dumpy little kid, and the kids called me 'Tank,' and I wasn't very good. I played middle guard, but I just wasn't ready to play with those guys. But they'd let me get in for the last few minutes. We had a good team. My father would always be there. Sometimes Jimmy and my mother would be there. Larry played on that team, and Daryle played on another team. If we played our games at different times, my folks would run from one game to another. My dad loved sports, but he didn't really push us. He never made us play, but he liked it when we did. He wasn't one of those guys running around telling the coach how to run things. I guess one time he did say something to a coach.

"It was my senior year in high school, and I hadn't been able to practice much because of a pulled muscle. I remember it was a real hot night and I was playing both ways and didn't do very much. They pretty much stopped me cold, and I gained about thirty yards. Raymond came in near the end of the game and almost broke it open and we almost won the game. I guess my father thought Raymond should have been in there earlier so he asked the coach why Raymond didn't play more. But I believe that was the only time he said anything to anybody.

"One time he did run down to the sidelines, but he didn't jump on the coach. Larry was playing at Linden McKinley High and his team was behind by a touchdown and he got hurt. Everybody figured Linden might win if Larry could get back in there, so my daddy ran down and told him to get back in. He did and ran eighty-five yards for a touchdown. My daddy's just the kind of man who believes in working hard and doing the very best you can with the talent God has given you. None of us has ever wanted to disappoint him because he's really lived for us."

A visitor to the Griffin home might get the impression that Papa Griffin has the same ideas about discipline as did his father but that he tempers it with a great deal of love—and that he's the iron hand in the velvet glove. Not so.

"I guess lots of people figure my daddy makes all the decisions, but my mother's not bashful. She's pretty quiet until she gets to know you or trusts someone, but she's strong. Believe me, she's plenty strong. My daddy has worked three and four jobs for so many years that he wasn't home all that much, so a lot of the discipline fell to my mother. She handled it all right. You couldn't take advantage of her."

Archie's earliest memories are of the house and store on Rich Street. Those were the grade school years. The houses in that area are packed tightly together, and the neighborhood has fallen victim to urban decay.

There is not a single unhappy memory of the place for Archie Griffin.

"Looking back, I know we were poor, but no poorer than any of my friends who lived there. I guess I didn't realize we didn't have much. We had the store, and us kids helped Mom in there. My daddy was working all the time even then, and he didn't spend much time in the store. I remember I used to take pop and sweets out of there. I've always been big on sweets. Maybe that's why I was so fat when I was a little boy."

It struck Archie Griffin as odd that as he was pulling the luxury automobile that professional football had enabled him to drive into the old neighborhood, he recalled the long distances he used to walk in other days.

"It doesn't seem like very far now, but back then I remember going just a few blocks, and it seemed like a long way. And on Sunday, after church, some of us would walk all the way down-

town and go to the show at the Southern Theatre. It cost just a
dime then. It was cheaper on Sundays. It seemed like it took forever to walk there back then, but now it doesn't seem that far to
me. We went to church at the Caldwell Temple. It's been torn
down now. A lot of buildings have been torn down, and some
others have been boarded up. It looks kinda bleak now, but we
had fun. That's about all I remember, having fun."

Griffin's Grocery later became Mac's Grocery, but the sign that
used to advertise coneys, cosmetics, hosiery, and ice cream is
weatherbeaten. The store is boarded up, and you can't buy any
groceries at all on the corner of Rich and Carpenter streets. The
Griffins lived in one side of the store and later moved into quarters upstairs. The streets are narrow, barely wide enough for cars
to pass.

Just down the street is Blackburn Park. There's a nice recreation center there now with all the proper facilities, but when
Archie was growing up the only facilities were the outside kind.

"We kept that place busy. We played so hard there the grass
wouldn't grow. I remember we played a game called 'Smear the
Queer.' I didn't even know what a queer was. We'd get a bunch
of guys and just throw a football in the air, and then tackle who-
ever got it. You really got smeared in that game, but it was fun.
Raymond was younger than I was, but he'd always beat me when
we'd race. I was fat, and he'd beat me every time. It really made
me mad."

It has often been said of the Griffins that their toughest competition came not from their teammates, but from members of their
own family.

"I'm sure my older brothers would have done just as well as I
did if they could have gone to a larger school, and it's true that we
had great competition within the family. For example, I think
Raymond would have done as well, or better, had he played
offense at Ohio State. He wanted to play so badly that when he
was a freshman he volunteered to go on defense. And he's been so
good at it they can't move him now."

Archie himself might never have become a running back had it not been for an experience in church league football.

"I played for the Maryland AC team for two years, then we moved out to the north end of Columbus, and I played for another team, called Caldwell Temple. It was in the same league as Maryland. I was still playing guard, but one day none of the fullbacks showed up for practice, and the coaches tried me. I guess I was twelve then. I never went back to the line again. We played nine games a year. We had good equipment, and a lot of people came to see us. When I say a lot, I don't mean thousands. But we had a couple of hundred people come out to see us when we played on Sunday afternoons. I remember the best game I had. I gained about 180 yards playing against my old teammates from Maryland."

Archie had learned to discipline himself a couple of seasons before that. It was then he found out just how much football mattered.

"There were certain weights prescribed for the seventh- and eighth-grade teams, so I had to lose a lot of weight. I did some weird things to do it. I'd get those plastic bags from the dry cleaners and I'd wrap myself up in them and I'd sweat so much the plastic would melt. Then we had an old car in the back. The tires were flat and all the windows were out of it, but it'd still be pretty hot out there in that car on a summer day. So I'd get in there and push the seats down. I'd do pushups and situps and all sorts of exercises.

"I guess I was twelve then and I weighed 135 pounds. That meant I had to lose 10 pounds. My mother knew what I was doing. Maybe she thought I was goofy, but she didn't stop me. I'd get in the bathroom and turn on all the hot water and put towels by the door so the steam couldn't get out. I'd do jumping jacks and more exercises in there. Of course, I cut down on food, too. But finally I lost the weight so I could play. It was wild, though.

"I remember at Caldwell my number was 32. My hero was Jim Brown. I wanted to be just like him. I used to love the way he could break tackles, and he had a funny way of getting off the ground. He got up real slow, like he was dying. Then he'd come back the next play and tear it up again. He took some shots, but he always gave more than he got. I remember the best feeling I had was at a banquet, at the Caldwell Temple Church, and I was in the eighth grade. The coach introduced me as the next Jim Brown. I didn't say anything, but it sure made me feel good. For a long time when we'd mess around playing football in a pickup game, I'd get the ball and say, 'Hey, I'm Jim Brown.' Other kids had their favorite players, but Jim Brown was all mine. I was really proud to have his number.

"I remember all the numbers I've had. At Maryland AC I wore No. 13. I didn't even know 13 was supposed to be an unlucky number back then. When I got to Eastmoor High I wore No. 33, but in my senior year there was a foulup and they didn't make a No. 33, so when the new jerseys came out I got No. 35. At Ohio State they gave me No. 45, and I've had that ever since. If someone at the Bengals had been using that one, I wouldn't have asked for it. No way."

It would have been totally out of character for Archie to ask a special favor. It's something they learned at home. James and Margaret Griffin rarely had to punish any of the children.

"They're all good children," said Mrs. Griffin, "and I'm not just saying that because they're mine. But we really haven't ever had any trouble with any of them. They're all different, I guess, but in many ways they're the same. Jimmy, the oldest, wasn't hard to handle. He had to take on a lot of responsibility early and help out in the store, help out around the house, and help out with the younger children. As for Archie, it seemed he was always active, always playing, always doing something. He never could just sit. He was forever on the go. He loved to sleep, though. I guess he was worn out from playing so hard.

"When folks were saying he was too small to make it at Ohio State, I just knew that he could make it. Maybe that's what you call mother instinct, but I had a special feeling about it. We've al-

21. *Above left,* Another record tumbled on this thirty-yard run, when Archie got loose against Illinois on November 8, 1975, and broke the NCAA mark for most consecutive games over the hundred-yard rushing standard. 22. *Above right,* This was the scene at the home finale at Ohio Stadium in Columbus on November 15, 1975, and Coach Woody Hayes came out onto the field to congratulate the man he's called the finest player and best human being he's ever coached. 23. *Right,* There weren't many glorious Rose Bowl moments for Ohio State, but this was one of them. Archie lifted quarterback Cornelius Greene into the air after Corny scored against Southern California in the 1975 Rose Bowl game at Pasadena.

24. *Top,* Archie and Loretta Griffin. 25. *Middle,* First one for pay—Archie Griffin scored his first professional football touchdown on this play against the Green Bay Packers. 26. *Bottom,* Archie didn't see as much daylight in his first season in the NFL as he had seen in college, but his coach says things will improve right away.

27. *Above left*, Archie with proud parents Margaret and James Griffin, Sr. 28. *Above right*, Archie working with some kids—those less fortunate. 29. *Right*, Mama Griffin and Archie.

long ago I went out for a walk at six o'clock in the morning. About five out of six cars that passed me had just one person in them. We've become so fragmented. You don't even see any big movie houses any longer. They've split them up into a bunch of little movie houses. People don't get together anymore and do anything with a community interest and community spirit. When Khrushchev was over here in 1959 he remarked about the Golden Gate Bridge. Someone asked him what he meant, and he said 'What a waste, one person in each car.' And he was right. Now, with our fuel shortage, maybe we'll have more people in one car and we can all get to know one another again.

"Even our football players move out of the dormitories as soon as we allow them to. They get into apartments because they want to be off by themselves when they should be in the dorms getting to know other people better. Our automobiles are not even made for courting girls any more. I don't know whether you know that or not, but it's true. Families don't hold together. Churches don't hold together. Communities don't hold together. We don't have those old-fashioned Saturday socials any longer, and about the only time older and younger people get together is at weddings and funerals. It's a shame, a real shame. That's why the Griffins stick out so much. They're real examples for good in so many ways, and that's why I want Arch to get a law degree and go into politics. The world needs more leaders like Arch."

Coach Hayes is delighted that Archie Griffin has become a hero to so many young people.

"We don't have many heroes nowadays, and sometimes if we do they're the wrong kind. I remember as a kid I had two heroes. One of them was Walter Johnson, the old-timer pitcher. I used to go down to Denver Reed's Smoke House to pick up my newspapers for delivery, and old Cy Young would be there talking about Walter Johnson.

"Then there was my dad, Wayne Benton Hayes. He was the most educated man I ever knew. He put everything he ever knew to use. He was a terrific teacher. He maintained that if a teacher

27. *Above left,* Archie with proud parents Margaret and James Griffin, Sr. 28. *Above right,* Archie working with some kids—those less fortunate. 29. *Right,* Mama Griffin and Archie.

30. *Top*, Archie Griffin accepting his second Heisman Trophy. 31. *Bottom*, A round of applause for Mr. and Mrs. Griffin at the Heisman ceremonies.

ways thought all of our children would be successful and could do anything they made up their minds to do. When Archie was having to make the decision about college, he told me he hadn't given much thought to Ohio State. The two things that convinced him were meeting Coach Hayes, and his father hinting that it might not be a bad idea to go to Ohio State. Archie felt that's where his father wanted him to go. I wanted him to go to Ohio State all along. But neither his father nor I told him where to go. I'm sure he took our feelings into consideration, but I know he's glad he went there."

Coach Woody Hayes makes it a point of recruiting not just good athletes, but also good parents.

"The Griffins are the greatest family you'll ever meet," Hayes says. "That's why Arch has been so great. I'll tell you, I've seen more love and respect in that home than in almost any I've ever witnessed. They're what a family is all about.

"You know, this is exactly why I can't buy this women's lib stuff. These kids need to be taken care of before they can even toddle. It's being proved all the time, taking a child back to the first hours it comes into the world. In your war-torn areas they rescue these youngsters—kids who don't have the advantage of having a mother, maybe she's been killed or something—but we rescue that child and feed it and bathe it and clean it up and give it a nice crib, but it'll develop withdrawal symptoms and within twenty-one days it will die. Now, this happens if those kids don't get good treatment right in the beginning. You go talk to your leading psychiatrists and pediatricians and this is becoming more and more prevalent in their thinking. It's no good for the mother to be away from the home.

"The Griffins have had a lot of love, and that's why they'll be successful in whatever they do, and that's why they are such happy people. They're well adjusted. They don't let any problems get to be big problems. They're a real team.

"And you know, we've always pulled entirely away from the team concept in this country. Why, when I was in Chicago not long ago I went out for a walk at six o'clock in the morning. About five out of six cars that passed me had just one person in them. We've become so fragmented. You don't even see any big movie houses any longer. They've split them up into a bunch of little movie houses. People don't get together anymore and do anything with a community interest and community spirit. When Khrushchev was over here in 1959 he remarked about the Golden Gate Bridge. Someone asked him what he meant, and he said 'What a waste, one person in each car.' And he was right. Now, with our fuel shortage, maybe we'll have more people in one car and we can all get to know one another again.

"Even our football players move out of the dormitories as soon as we allow them to. They get into apartments because they want to be off by themselves when they should be in the dorms getting to know other people better. Our automobiles are not even made for courting girls any more. I don't know whether you know that or not, but it's true. Families don't hold together. Churches don't hold together. Communities don't hold together. We don't have those old-fashioned Saturday socials any longer, and about the only time older and younger people get together is at weddings and funerals. It's a shame, a real shame. That's why the Griffins stick out so much. They're real examples for good in so many ways, and that's why I want Arch to get a law degree and go into politics. The world needs more leaders like Arch."

Coach Hayes is delighted that Archie Griffin has become a hero to so many young people.

"We don't have many heroes nowadays, and sometimes if we do they're the wrong kind. I remember as a kid I had two heroes. One of them was Walter Johnson, the old-timer pitcher. I used to go down to Denver Reed's Smoke House to pick up my newspapers for delivery, and old Cy Young would be there talking about Walter Johnson.

"Then there was my dad, Wayne Benton Hayes. He was the most educated man I ever knew. He put everything he ever knew to use. He was a terrific teacher. He maintained that if a teacher ever flunked a student it was a downright sin, a sin against the teacher for failing to motivate the pupil.

"I've been a hero worshiper all my life. I loved Gene Tunney because he was much smarter than Jack Dempsey. Besides, Tunney had a great war record, and Dempsey was a draft dodger. Tunney was handsome, and the way he fought was even prettier. He really practiced the manly art of self-defense.

"Everybody knows I've been a great admirer of General George Patton. He was a great warrior and a great strategist. He had a great sense of history. Besides, I was in the war, and I know quite a bit about it from the inside. I had command of two ships. I recall when I went back to coaching after the war, my alma mater, Denison, gave me my first college coaching opportunity. They asked me if I thought my experience as a commanding officer would help me as a football coach. I said, 'Maybe, but my experience as a football coach certainly helped me as a commanding officer.' I mean, you have to have discipline and respect, and you have to be able to sense when something isn't right.

"The man at the top has to be able to make decisions. What Harry Truman said about the buck stopping right here is true. He was an interesting person. I admired him. He came up through the biggest crook machine they had, but it never seemed to touch him. He was above it. Just like the late Mayor Daley in Chicago. He did the best job in the country, yet you know he pulled the crookedest deal in the world when he threw the election to Kennedy in 1960.

"I have a great deal of respect for that German field marshal, Irwin Rommel. He was truly a great leader. He just was on the wrong side, that's all. He knew what was wrong with the German situation. I couldn't believe it for years that he had been critical of Hitler and was part of that deal to get him out. He just didn't sound like a plotter, but above everything else he had a sense of what was right.

"All great people have that, and that's the major thing about the Griffins. They know what is right. They do what is right all the time. Most things that happen to people can be traced back to their home life. I've been reading a book some professor wrote on the essence of self-esteem. It's one helluva tough book to read, but it's all about how a person is treated by his family. It's about how you're made to feel about yourself, and it's a reflected thing. You can call it corny if you want, but the things Archie Griffin talks about in his speeches—dedication, determination, and desire, the three *d*'s, as he calls them—they'll carry you through life's toughest battles."

It was a counselor at Linmoor Junior High School who first told Archie about the three *d*'s.

"His name was Oscar Gill," Archie recalled. "I really learned a lot in junior high school. It was fun. Life was carefree and there was no responsibility, but it was a good learning experience for me, too. I think junior high school is the time you really start to learn, and the time when you get the feeling whether you're going to make it in life or not. I was elected president of the Student Council in the ninth grade. I guess the kids liked me some, because I didn't do any campaigning for the thing. But I remember when Mr. Gill sat a bunch of us down and talked to us about dedication, determination, and desire. It's stayed with me all this time, and I just know those things will be with me forever."

Tom Pinckney and Wayne Bell and Bobby Saunders and Paul Robinson and Tony Harrison were among Archie's good buddies at Linmoor Junior High School. Some of them formed singing groups, and twice tried to win local talent contests.

"The best we ever finished was second, though, so I decided I better stick with football."

Papa Griffin instructed all his children early on never to start trouble, and never to get involved in other people's business.

"I don't think any of us ever got in many fights. I remember just a couple of times when I had a little scrape or two. There was a fellow in the eighth grade, his name was Ted Callahan, and I guess he wanted to see who had the most power in his class. People would ask me if I could beat Teddy, and I'd tell them I didn't know. When they asked him if he could beat me, he'd always say he could. He kept bothering me and testing me. I was walking down the hall one day with a guy named Carl Harris, and Teddy called me a pretty bad name. I let it pass.

"Then he called me the same thing a little while later and I was walking with my girl. Then all of a sudden he hit me and jumped at me. I hit him back, and he went down. I picked him up and threw him down, and a lot of guys came and pulled me off him. He never bothered me after that.

"There was another time I had a little bit of trouble. I was playing baseball in a park, and three guys started riding me. Finally one of them stepped in front of me. I was just gonna walk right on home. But he hit me with the heel of his hand on the back of my head. They kinda surrounded me, but there was an opening in the back. I turned and slapped one of the guys, and all I remember after that is running all the way home. I didn't see any point in trying to whip three of them. That was one time I didn't even have any interest in waiting around to turn the other cheek. If one of them was bold enough to think he could whip me by himself, I kept thinking what three of them would do to me. Running just seemed to be the smart thing to do."

The Griffins gradually outgrew the house on Duxberry in the Linden area of Columbus—but because of a lack of funds, they lived in it quite a number of years after they had done the outgrowing. The house has two bedrooms, a basement, a little recreation room, and an attic where the Griffins stacked some beds.

"Jimmy, Larry, Daryle, and I slept upstairs. Raymond and Duncan had one room downstairs, and I guess Keith slept in there with them. My folks and Crystal slept in another room, and the rest of us slept upstairs. It was pretty crowded, to say the least."

Almost since he came to Columbus, James Griffin has worked two jobs and sometimes three to feed and clothe his brood. Before the sun rises, he's on the job for the Columbus City Sanitation Department. Once that full-time job is over in midafternoon, he heads for a full shift of work at the Ohio Malleable Company.

When quitting time comes at eleven o'clock at night, more nights than not James Griffin, Sr., then scoots out to either a school or a private company where he has a part-time custodial job.

"He's unbelievable. I've never understood how he keeps going. I remember sometimes when I was little, he'd pile us kids into a car on one of his nights off and take us all to a drive-in movie. He'd fall asleep as soon as he parked the car. The man has amazing endurance. All of us want him to slow down, but he won't hear anything about it. Maybe when Keith gets out of high school he'll give up one of his jobs. I've tried to talk him into slowing down and the rest of the boys have talked to him, too. But he's the boss."

When Archie was finishing his junior high school studies the Griffins moved into a bigger, better home on the east side of town. As quickly as Archie established himself as an extraordinary football performer, the rumor mill ground out two different versions of why the Griffins moved. The first story was that supporters of the Eastmoor High School program had arranged to purchase the house for the Griffins. The second rumor was that the National Association for the Advancement of Colored People had arranged for the Griffins to move into the Berwick area as part of a "block busting" campaign into predominantly white neighborhoods.

"I didn't hear any of those rumors until much later, but I can guarantee you that neither one of them is true. My daddy worked hard and saved his money to make a down payment on a better and bigger house for his family so we all could have a little better life. And that's the only story that has any truth to it."

The new area was predominantly white, and Archie would be a sophomore and Daryle a junior in a mostly white high school, Eastmoor.

"It was quite a change for me. I'd never really been around a lot of whites because all the neighborhoods I had lived in were mostly black, and the schools had been mostly black. We moved in May, and I spent most of that first summer back in the old neighborhood with my friends."

Archie did not even play junior high school football. His school had no football program, so he played basketball and ran track. But there was no question he'd be going out for the football team at Eastmoor. After all, it was a family tradition. And all the brothers preceding him had made the team as sophomores.

Bob Stuart remembers the first time he saw Archie Griffin.

"He and his brother walked onto the field the first day of practice before the fall season, and someone said they were the Griffin brothers. They weren't that big, and I didn't notice Archie as much as I did his older brother: I remembered him from the previous season—he had broken a long run to beat us in a critical game. I guess Archie caught my eye during our late-summer conditioning drills. We did a lot of sprinting, and he was consistently running 4.5 and 4.6 in the 40-yard dashes, and that's pretty spectacular. And he had that look about him that said he was a good athlete. Sometimes you can just look at a guy and see something special. We knew he had speed, but speed alone isn't enough. We really didn't know what we had, but we planned to find out."

Bob Stuart is a fifty-two-year-old high school football coach who's never had another head coaching job. In fact, he's the only coach Eastmoor has ever had. His teams have won seven city championships, and if Keith Griffin pans out as everyone, including Coach Stuart figures, there'll be more as he begins his twenty-second season this year.

The Griffins can talk all they want about Keith's potential, but for Bob Stuart, there'll never be another quite like Archie:

"We figured to have a fine team that year, and we already had an outstanding tailback in Brian King. Matter of fact, we thought he'd be the best in the city. I guess we had worked in pads and scrimmaged only a couple of times when Archie came up to me as we were leaving the field one day and said, 'Coach, what do I have to do to start?' Now, he said in a searching, not boastful way. He never was cocky, from the first day I met him. He just wanted to know. I don't recall my exact words to him, but I told him just to keep doing the things he was doing. He was really hitting people.

"We had five men on our coaching staff, and all of us were talking about Archie. We kept having two-a-day workouts, and every workout Archie would simply stand out. He was a real worker. Other guys would stop a couple of yards upfield after a play, but Archie—he'd keep running. I don't think I ever saw anybody work harder and give more of himself. He hustled every minute.

"As the season began, we had decided to alternate Archie with Brian, but before the season was too far along it became apparent we just couldn't keep Archie out of there. He was unbelievable. He gained something like 750 yards as a sophomore, and he just kept getting better. In Archie's junior year, we lost our opening game and then won the rest. When he was a senior, we lost one game but won the city championship. And I know, in the last three games of his career, he played with tremendous pain. In fact, I wouldn't be surprised if he played with some broken bones in his foot. He was really hobbling, but we had two critical games coming up, the first one against our biggest rival, Walnut Ridge. He must have gained 180 yards on traps, and he limped every step of the way. When we played Linden McKinley for the city championship, he just had to be in awful pain, but he never complained at all. Most guys would have headed right for the tub, but not Archie. He just tore 'em up."

Stuart has vivid memories of that title game. It was to be played at ten o'clock in the morning.

"We didn't want the kids to be drowsy or sluggish, so we told the parents to get 'em up early, and we planned a big breakfast at the school at seven o'clock. My wife, Betty, was helping serve the breakfast, and so was Archie's mother. Mrs. Griffin told Betty she didn't think Archie would ever come downstairs that morning. But he wasn't sleeping. He was up there praying."

Stuart confesses he never taught Archie Griffin a single thing in those three years.

"It might sound better to say I helped develop this particular skill, or showed him some dandy move, or that I helped mold his character or helped shape his personality, but the truth of the matter is that Archie came to us as a made football player and a made human being. He'd run at someone rather than go for the sidelines. We used to sit and pray for him to get someone in a one-on-one situation. Archie'd beat the guy every time. Sometimes he'd beat the guy just by intimidation. That'll happen sometimes, no matter whether you're playing grade school or pro football. There are some guys who, when faced by a tremendous athlete, will give it what I call 'the great avoid,' and Archie'd make guys do that.

"He was simply phenomenal. I never had to get on him one time, not for anything. He led by quiet example. He never got out of line a single time. He's a person of great character, and his influence on others is staggering. He practiced hurt, he played hurt, and I never heard him utter a single complaint about anything. He either was born with, or developed early an unusual ability to make a determination when to stop and when to go. He knew when to attack and how to use his speed and strength. A lot of people thought he just had speed, but he's a bull of a runner and a lot stronger than people think.

"Archie always had this great capacity to read the entire field. He could read the flow of the play, both on offense and defense, and he had this great sense of anticipation. He could always find the seams in the defense. On top of all that, he had a ton of courage. That's something you can never measure in a person, but it stuck out all over him."

Stuart will not say he had a particularly close relationship with Archie.

"I would have liked for him to be closer, but the Griffins aren't that way. They're not stuffy, and they're not aloof. It's just that they're, well, you might say snuggly in their own family relationship, that they don't get close to many other people. Some kids will bug you and others will blow smoke, but Archie was very much his own person. He didn't talk a whole lot, but if he had a question or a comment he got right to it. He didn't waste words. My relationship with him was really good, and still is, and I think we've always had this mutual respect. I don't think I've ever had more respect for an athlete."

The Griffins came to Eastmoor at the height of the black uprising, when blacks were openly critical of the educational system. The black students complained that schools were not addressing themselves to black history, black problems, and were not sensitive to black needs. There were protests and boycotts, not just at Eastmoor but also all across the land. On more than one occasion at Eastmoor, black students congregated in the gymnasium and refused to go to class until they were assured their complaints would be heard. And where were the Griffins during all this?

"They stayed away from the problems," Stuart recalled. "They simply got along with everybody. They weren't really loners. They just gave you straight talk on everything. I know one time I asked Archie why he was not joining in the protest, and he said, 'I always ask my father what to do, and he said he'd tell me what was right and what was wrong.' And that's exactly what he did. If they were criticized by other blacks for not participating actively, I'm not aware of it."

"It wasn't a matter of not getting involved," Archie remembers. "There wasn't any sense in my screaming and yelling. I could understand why some people were upset, but I can honestly say I never felt discriminated against. I'll admit, when I moved into that end of town, I thought I was gonna have a lot of prejudice to contend with. But we never talked about it at home. My daddy didn't sit us all down around the table and say, 'Hey, now, we're moving into this new neighborhood and you're gonna have trouble.' It just wasn't talked about. And none of us had any trouble that I know of. I was in school to get an education, and hopefully to get a scholarship to go to college to take some of the financial burdens off my daddy.

"Sure, I was afraid someone would call me a nigger or something. But if they ever did, it was behind my back. As soon as school started and the season began, I made lots of new friends. For the first time in my life, I had some good white friends, too. I became good friends with the McKelvey brothers, Gary and Tom. Tom and I kinda hung together. Then there were the Cohens; Jeff was my age and Gary a year younger. They were Jewish. They were on the wrestling team with me, and we got along great. There were lots of Jewish guys on our football team. But nothing mattered. I didn't look for trouble, and I didn't find any. Most all my teachers were white. I had one black teacher in a black studies class. I guess I didn't go around thinking in terms of color, and I don't think any of my friends did, either."

Archie Griffin didn't dodge the tough courses any more than he did tough assignments on the field.

Coach Stuart: "I remember talking with Archie about some of the tough courses he was taking. He took some of the really tough courses even though he knew he wouldn't do as well in them. I remember he took a physics course and got a "D" in it. But he told me he figured he needed it for college. He was very dedicated academically and he had tough, demanding teachers. He didn't get any favors in the classroom."

Archie wound up with a 2.7-point average out of a possible 4 points.

Even during his high school days, and every year since then, Coach Stuart has called on Archie to help out with some problem athletes.

"He had this tremendous influence, and once in a while you'll get a kid who's jiving around and getting into some trouble. I've frequently gone to Archie and asked him if he'd just speak to a particular young man. And he always does it, and he does it with such class. And a fellow who used to play for us at Eastmoor had been doing some student teaching down in southwestern Ohio and he was having a lot of difficulty with a pair of brothers. These kids were great athletes, but they were goofing off so much they were about to get booted out of school. So Greg [Miller] talked with me about it and asked if I thought it'd be all right for him to call Archie. Now, here was Archie, down in Cincinnati, in the middle of his rookie season in pro football and busier than the dickens with his own life, but when Greg called him you can't believe what happened. Well, you can believe it if you know Archie like I do.

"Archie got tickets to one of the Bengals' home games, had the teacher and the two boys come into the locker room after the game and then Archie took the two boys aside. He told them they had better be getting their act together. I'm sure he told them about dedication, determination, and desire, like he always does. But you know something wonderful? That always works. Archie's such a hero, and has such impact, that you can't believe it. I talked later with the student teacher, and he told me these boys had done an amazing about-face. He said they were so good now butter wouldn't melt in their mouths. And all because of Archie Griffin. I've coached thousands of young people for a lot of years, and I can truthfully say I've never met a finer young man than Archie. I guess he has more of a conscience than anyone I've ever met."

Stuart remembers the agonizing Archie did over his choice of a college, and his recollection differs somewhat from that of his old friend Woody Hayes.

"Here's another case where it might be nice to say Archie left things in my hands and that I had a great influence on him, but the decision was made by Archie himself. I'm sure he considered his family's wishes above everything else, but it was something he put a lot of thought into, like he did everything else. There's never anything haphazard about Archie's decisions.

"He came to me one day and asked if I thought we could talk to the coach at Northwestern. He'd sort of made up his mind that's where he wanted to go to school. Up to that time—and this was right at the tail end of his senior year—Ohio State hadn't really recruited him aggressively. They'd had some graduate assistants out to watch him play and they had looked at some game films, but they hadn't really come after him. Well, I went right to the telephone and called Alex Agase, who was coaching at Northwestern then.

"Our school wouldn't let us make phone calls for things like that, so I had to call Agase collect, and he accepted the call even though I'd never met him. I told him about Archie, and you know what, he was right there at Eastmoor High School the next day. He had a long talk with Archie about going to Northwestern, and they really wanted him.

"Like I said, Ohio State hadn't really made any strong overture. Rudy Hubbard was an assistant coach then and he had done some student teaching with me at Eastmoor and he knew more about Archie than anyone up there. So I called Rudy and told him, 'If you people are interested in Archie Griffin, you'd better get your stuff together.' I had promised him I'd keep him posted.

"All Archie ever asked me about college was if I thought he could play at Northwestern. I told him very candidly he could play wherever he went. He really didn't know how fine an athlete he was. Well, sir, Woody Hayes was experimenting with the wishbone offense at Ohio State at about that time, and for some reason Archie didn't care for that. He told me he just couldn't see himself in that type of situation. But right away, here came Woody out to Eastmoor. He took Archie aside, and they must have spent a couple of hours together. At that time, they had Morris Bradshaw as their big running back. He had just been shifted to tailback, and it looked like he'd set the world on fire. He'd averaged better than five yards a carry from right halfback the previous year, and he busted some long runs and maybe that was why they weren't all hopped up on Archie. Maybe they figured they were set at his position and really didn't need him. But when they found out Northwestern was high on him, they got it in gear.

"I don't know the sequence of events from then on, but on different occasions Archie'd come to me and say, 'Coach, are you sure I could really play up there at Ohio State?,' and I'd tell him the same thing I told him at the beginning, that he could play anyplace in the world if he wanted to. He never once asked me for my opinion as to what he should do, but I told him one time if it came down to a decision and he couldn't pick one school over the other, that maybe it'd be a good idea to go with a winner. I just thought Archie was the greatest thing since sliced bread, and I knew in my heart he could excel wherever he went."

That made three people who were certain of that at that point: the coach and the Griffin parents.

Looking back, about all Archie remembers was some apprehension.

"I just wanted to play. Every time I've gone out for any team, my first goal is to make the squad. I really never gave much thought to playing right away. I figured I'd be on the bench for quite a while. For a long time up there, I was way down the list. They had some really good players, and I figured it'd be a while before I'd play."

But the opportunity to play came right away, and Archie Griffin quickly bolted to stardom at a school known for producing larger-than-life football heroes. He was lauded by the media, lionized by the fans, and loved by the students. Everybody, everywhere, knew of Archie Griffin, No. 45. Everyone except Loretta Laffitte. She not only had not heard of Archie Griffin, but also didn't care to hear about him, nor about anyone else who played football for Ohio State.

"I just plain didn't like Ohio State football," said Loretta. "I lived in Lincoln Towers, right by the football stadium. I hated football Saturdays. We had to get up and out of there by seven o'clock in the morning or we were simply locked in. We had to get the cars out of the parking lot so they could use the lot for football parking. Anything to make more money for Ohio State. It used to really make my blood boil. After all, we had paid fees to park there, yet we had to move them or they'd tow them away. So I hated everything connected with Ohio State football, and I mean I hated it with a passion."

They were finally thrown together in a math class when both were sophomores. Even though Loretta paid no attention to Archie before that, he surely had noticed her.

"I used to go around near where she lived and I noticed her all the time," he said. "She and the other ladies were always trying to get us to come to one of their social functions so they could make money, and I thought about asking her out, but she seemed like she wasn't interested."

Finally, he employed the age-old "Why don't we study for a test together?" trick a few weeks into the math class.

By that time, Loretta said she was aware of his celebrity status.

"We used to talk about him all the time because he was late for class once in a while. One day I said something about him being late again, and someone yelled at me and said, 'Don't you know who that is?' I said I didn't, and they said, 'Well, girl, that's Archie Griffin, the football star.' That's how I found out who he was, but I still didn't get impressed. This fan of his went on and on, raving about how great Archie was, and so I told him what I thought of Ohio State football. We really got into it."

Archie denies he was habitually tardy to class.

"First off, it was an eight-o'clock class, and I had to come all the way across campus. Loretta could jump out of bed and practically be in the classroom. Besides, I wasn't late that often."

He does not, however, deny making the first move.

"We had this test, and all but about two students flunked it. So we got to take it over, so I said to her, 'Maybe we'd better get together and study for this thing.' So Loretta and her girlfriend Kathy and I, we all got together and studied. From then on, I was hooked on her. The next quarter, we had another class together, so we were together a lot. But she was tough, I'll tell you that. I don't think she trusted me. She had this hangup about athletes."

Loretta doesn't deny that. "I was tired of everybody telling me about this big-time football player. I thought he would try to run a game on me, and I wasn't having any of that. But every time we'd see each other he'd be so nice and all, but I still held my feelings back because my daddy had warned me about big stars like that."

Looking back, they laugh heartily about the early days of their courtship, Archie saying, "She tried to be so tough all the time. She used to make me mad with that tough business. I couldn't even get her to kiss me. It was tough on the old ego, because I really dug her and I didn't know if the feeling was mutual."

It was, though, and they got married on June 26, 1976, not long after Archie's graduation and just before he was to report to the College All-Star camp in Chicago. They agree there were many, many factors to consider, perhaps more than in an ordinary marriage. They gave it a lot of thought.

"First, I know I could never have married someone who was not a Christian, and by that I mean a totally committed individual. I'm sure that's the big thing Loretta and I have in common. She's a good person in addition to being pretty. That meant a whole lot."

For Loretta, there were other factors to consider, mainly how she'd handle being married to a superstar. Marriage has become a high-risk proposition anyway, and the risks are greater when one of the partners is in a high-profile situation.

"A lot of people talked about the pressure on Archie and all that, but I feel there's more pressure on me. The wife of a superstar has a lot of problems built into the relationship. There are so many demands on his time and so much praise given him that the wife, well, she just has to be stronger than all the other people tugging at her man. You have to try and not let the outside people and things get you down, because if you let them, those outside things will destroy you. But you know in front you're gonna have to share the man, that's all there is to it. You just have to face it, and prepare yourself to handle it.

"Being at Ohio State with Archie helped get me used to that. Nothing can be as bad as that. I don't think it'll be more difficult now that he's in professional football. Being that Archie is from Columbus, and him going to Ohio State where they dote on their teams and players so much—well, the pressure was unbelievable. He was almost a god. I had funny phone calls, at all hours of the night. I don't mean funny ha-ha, I mean funny, like crazy phone calls. The worst thing was standing outside the locker room waiting for him to come out after a game. People would literally knock me out of the way just to get close to him. His life wasn't his own, and we had very little time to ourselves. It's a wonder we made it.

"I have a very short temper, and sometimes it was all I could do to control myself and to keep from telling people off. Sometimes I wanted to scream out and turn around and punch someone, but I never did. But I wanted to, that's for sure."

Recent surveys show that the football hero isn't the big man on campus he used to be, and that coeds now have as much respect for brains as for brawn.

That may be true at many places, but at Ohio State, a football star still becomes almost a folk hero. As for girls, Archie could have had almost his pick of the litter, but he had eyes only for Loretta from the very beginning.

"I know lots of girls just threw themselves at Archie, and they probably will as long as he plays football and is well known. But ever since we've been going together, he's spent all his spare time with me. I don't have time to worry about that kind of stuff. A girl who's married to someone like Archie has to be sure of herself. And she has to be sure of her man, too. And I'm sure of Archie. I just don't think Archie would ever do anything to hurt me.

"If there's ever been anybody else, she's gotten the short end of the stick, because every time there was a chance for me to go somewhere with him, he'd take me. There are people out there who might want to come between us, but they're not gonna do anything for Archie, and I am. Just like he does things for me."

Like what, for example?

"When he's not making a living, he's here. He loves me, and he cares about me. He provides for me. We do things together. My family is in Cleveland, so Archie is my family now. If I'm lonely, he understands. I can talk to him. We share lots of things."

What they do not share is a fanatic love for the game of football. Loretta likes it only if Archie is playing, or if she is familiar with some of the players on other teams. On the other hand, when Archie is home and there's a football game on television, he'd watch if there were two church league teams taking part.

"But he'll always ask if there's something I'd rather watch," Loretta cautions, "and if one of my favorite programs is on, Archie will watch football on another television set upstairs. He's considerate that way."

Most American husbands follow the same pattern. They work, they come home, and sometimes they complain about a hard day at the plant or the office. If they're lucky, they have a wife who understands and will listen to his problems before telling him how the neighbor kids ran their bikes over the newly seeded lawn and that one of the teachers called about a problem at school with Jamie.

The legendary Ben Hogan called the golf course his "office," and race driver A. J. Foyt rarely consents to be interviewed while he's working on one of his cars. For the football player, the stadium is the office, and sometimes even stars have bad days.

Archie Griffin played in forty-six football games during his four-year career at Ohio State. Only a dozen times did he gain fewer than a hundred yards, so there weren't all that many off days. But when they came, it was Loretta who had the big job of lifting his spirits.

"There were some times that were not as good as others, but I can't really say Archie is the kind of person who brings his troubles home with him. He pretty much can put bad things behind him. There was only one time things really got to him, and that was in the game against Pittsburgh. You know, the one the Bengals lost in that terrible snowstorm. It pretty much knocked them out of the playoffs, and when he came home he just kept saying, 'I caught that pass, I caught that pass.' So I know he caught it, because Archie just wouldn't lie. And he doesn't complain much about anything. Even that time, he wasn't moping or anything. He was just upset."

Archie Griffin disdains labels of any kind. He refuses to be drawn into conversations about women's liberation and male chauvinism, but it's obvious he relishes the role of provider and protector.

"I don't believe a man should burden his wife with lots of problems he may have at work, whether he works in football or in a factory. If there's something bugging a man and bothering him, then probably it's a good idea to share it with his mate so she can understand the problems. But as for coming home and unloading on your wife, well, I just think there are certain things a man should try to work out for himself."

Archie and Loretta bought a four-bedroom home before their marriage, but Archie spent precious little time in it for the first six months. First, it was the College All-Star camp, then training camp for the Bengals, and then the regular season. It was almost Christmas before they really settled in as married folks. During the season, Archie and one of his teammates stayed in an apartment in Cincinnati, and Loretta busied herself furnishing their home on the east side of Columbus and drove to Cincinnati for weekends when the Bengals were at home. On occasional off days, Archie would drive back to Columbus to spend a day with his bride.

Archie and Loretta had long discussions before the marriage about what each wanted out of the union. They'd like to have two children of their own, but not until they adopt a child. Loretta told why:

"I've worked with underprivileged kids, some of them with some pretty heavy problems. There are so many kids who aren't even given a halfway chance in life. Everybody wants a new baby to adopt, but if a child gets to the age of two or three, nobody wants that child. So these kids just stay in these homes or centers, and the longer they stay there the less their chances for getting out. They just stay there, that's all, and they wind up having not very much of a life. I think that's sad. There are lots of people who can afford to take these children into their homes, and if they'd just do that and show them that life can be better, I think a lot of the problems of the world could be solved. Most of these so-called problem children don't need anything more than love and affection.

"We've already checked into it, and they told us you have to be married two years before they let you adopt one of these children. I guess that's to make certain your marriage is all right. So what we'd like to do is hold off having our own family until we can adopt one of these kids. The reason for that is that we want to have the adopted child in our home and show her the right kind of love, then there'll be none of that business of our own children saying something like, 'Mama, where'd she come from?' We want to make certain that a child we adopt will know in her heart she's been adopted because of love. Then when she gets older, we'd tell her all about it. I wouldn't want somebody else to tell her. We've talked it all over, and we think that's the right thing to do."

It is not surprising that Archie and Loretta have strong feelings about family decisions. The Griffin family concept is well known, and it does not differ all that much from the way the Laffittes raised their brood.

"We were punished, but we got explanations with the punishment. And if we thought any punishment or decision was injust, we could ask about it and talk it over. It wasn't like we had to sit there and just take it. We had good family discussions, and I believe in that kind of thing. I grew up being taught that I could express myself, that I could have opinions about things and the right to say what I think."

Archie says Loretta habitually exercises that right.

"Some folks don't like it because she says what she thinks. She's a strong woman. But that's one of the things I like about her. She's not a weak person. Anything but weak. Right off, that's the first thing that attracted me to her. I knew right away she was a strong lady. Maybe that's why I liked her, because she didn't fall all over me just because I was a football player. The more I got to know her, the more I could see she was a person of fine character.

Of course, I noticed she was good-looking, too. As a matter of fact, we'd be studying together sometimes and I'd find myself just sitting and staring at her. Now that we're married we really enjoy each other. We do lots of things together. That's why we want to wait a little bit before having children, because once we have kids, her time won't be her own. She'll be pretty well tied down."

Their home is not far from Mama and Papa Griffin. The Griffins make it a practice not to get too far away from the mother ship.

"I can drive there in four or five minutes, but sometimes I do some running in the mornings, so instead of running around the block or through a park or something, I just run over to their house," Archie says.

Archie Griffin neither smokes nor drinks and never permits himself to get out of condition, but he confesses that those who advocate strict dietary habits for prime health will cringe a bit when they learn about the things he eats.

"I eat just everything, and I especially love sweets. I eat lots of sweets, and I always have. I just can't seem to stay away from them. And I eat some fried foods, too. I know fish and poultry are supposed to be good for you, but I like meat. Eggs are supposed to be bad for you, but I eat lots of eggs. I love 'em with sausage."

As for fish, Archie neither wants to eat fish nor catch fish. Two of his old buddies from the Linden area, Tom Pinckney and Wayne Bell, were recalling the first time Archie went fishing. They took him to a lake near Zanesville, Ohio, and Archie quickly eliminated himself as a possible host for an outdoors hunting and fishing show.

"He wouldn't even put the worm on the hook," Tom Pinckney recalled. "He called it the 'nasty,' so we had to bait his hook for him."

Bell remembered Archie dangling the end of the line into the water beneath a rock and catching a bluegill. "He jerked it out of the water and it was flying all over the place, but do you think Archie would take the fish off the hook? Man, he wouldn't even touch the thing. We had to do everything for him. He was really funny."

Archie figures perhaps his dislike for "regular fish" comes from that experience, so when he eats fish today, it's the shellfish variety.

Both Archie and Loretta have some schooling they want to complete. Loretta needs just a few hours to complete her work for a bachelor's degree. Archie intends to pursue postgraduate studies but probably won't follow Coach Hayes' advice to become a lawyer, then a politician.

"He has always talked that up, but I'm just not that interested in politics. Now, as for law school, I'm gonna do that. It's not important right now whether I ever practice law, but I think it'd be challenging to go into law school and maybe get a degree because what I'd learn can really help me in any field I enter after football is over."

He has no schedule for his professional football career, except that he will play so long as he can be effective and at the same time enjoy the game.

"I've never thought it was gonna be my whole life. That's why I have budgeted myself and we're living on a set amount of money—the amount I figure I could make outside of football when I'm through playing. I'm planning on training for a career with some company. There have been some opportunities that have come up, and I'm planning on getting into something like that to prepare myself for the day when I'm through with football."

Would it not be fair to expect that any Griffin offspring would be excellent athletes? Archie says there are other things far more important than that.

"I'd hope our children would first be good, considerate human beings. People can talk all they want about what my brothers and I have done in sports, but they should remember first what kind of parents we have and how they've sacrificed so long for us. The home life is the important thing. Some of my brothers are all through with football. They were great players but now they're raising their families and contributing to a better life for everyone. Someday I'll be all through with football and my younger brothers will be through, and it's my hope people will remember us for more than that. Football has given all of us an education and maybe made life a lot easier for us, but life goes on without football.

"I'm gonna try to be like my father was. He never once pushed us into sports, and I don't think he had any idea when all this started we'd get this far with it. But he and my mother made certain we were raised in the right way. I just can't tell you how much of their own lives they gave up so us kids would have it a whole lot better than they did. My dad wanted to go to college and he couldn't, so he made up his mind that all his kids got a college education. If Loretta and I are blessed with children, our main job is to give them a good home and a lot of love. If they're good at sports, that'll be fine. But I won't push it. I will push them to be good citizens, though."

Archie has a wonderfully easy way with children. Once, at the Cincinnati Bengals' training camp at Wilmington, a young boy waited outside the locker-room facility for the players to emerge.

Greg Nard came to the Bengals' camp every day. His sixteen-year-old brother David had told him about Cincinnati's exciting new rookie, Archie Griffin. He told him how the two-time Heisman Trophy winner had taken time after practice to play a pickup basketball game with some teen-agers.

"I was a little afraid to say hello to him, but one day I just walked up and said, 'Hi.' He stopped and talked to me for a long time. So every day now I wait for him, and he always stops and talks to me."

"What do you talk about with Archie Griffin?"

"We just talk mainly about football."

"Do you know how great a player he is?"

"Yep. My brother told me about him at Ohio State. I asked Archie how he got to be so good."

"What did he say?"

"He said he wasn't all that good but the other players made him look good because they blocked so hard."

"Is it a big thrill for you to get to see him and talk with him?"

"No. I was pretty excited at first, and I used to talk to Isaac Curtis and some of the other players. They're all pretty nice guys. I'm used to it now so I don't get too excited about it. But I think Archie Griffin is gonna be my main man."

Archie remembers that little tyke, and lots of other like him. In an era when many sports stars won't take the time to sign an autograph, Archie has a policy he won't ever bend.

"I'm not trying to be a big deal or anything, but people make you what you are. I mean, you just have to be nice to people. That goes all the way back to the Bible, you know, that part about doing unto others as you'd have them do unto you. Kids are great. I've always wondered what kids think and feel when they come up to somebody they admire and they get the brushoff. What goes through their minds? They have a certain image of the player and maybe a special feeling about him, and all of a sudden all that is torn down because the athlete won't take the time to sign an autograph. I love kids. In fact, I just love people. I guess there have been times when it got a little hectic, but all in all, I just can't forget how great people have been to me, ever since I can remember."

Wherever he goes, Archie is like the Pied Piper.

It was twelve degrees below zero when he and Loretta walked into the morning worship service at the Bethel AME Church in Archie's old neighborhood in the Linden area. It is the same church he attended during his junior high school years. He remained active in church activities through his high school years and joined the fellowship of the church once he made a commitment to Jesus Christ.

The wind-chill factor of forty-seven degrees below zero held the usually good attendance down to some seventy parishioners. At Bethel AME Church, Archie is an old friend and a familiar face, and the young people, while still wide-eyed, are most respectful and grant the Griffins some degree of privacy.

"They've known me for so long I guess I'm just one more person here, and that's good. When I was in high school I gave a sermon here on youth day, then when I was a freshman in college I sang a duet with a girl here. I remember we sang 'Swing Low, Sweet Chariot.' Daryle gave a tremendous sermon here one time and talked about his involvement with the Fellowship of Christian Athletes. You know, one time Daryle was named Ohio's Christian Athlete of the Year by the FCA. He's a tremendous person, and he's been a great influence on me and the rest of the kids.

"The Reverend E. E. Jordan was the pastor here for a long time, and he had great impact on me. He was a tremendous man."

On this bitterly cold day the sixteen-voice choir at Bethel blended beautifully in leading the congregation in singing the familiar words:

> *Oh, for a thousand tongues to sing,*
> *My great Redeemer's praise,*
> *The glories of my God and King,*
> *The triumphs of his grace.*

Archie was familiar with every song sung that morning. He likes the old songs.

"I guess you could say I like what they call the old-time religion. I don't like much that's fancy. When I hear a sermon, I want to know where it comes from in the Bible. And I'd rather hear a man give a prayer from the heart than read something fancy off a piece of paper, you know, something he's written down ahead of time.

"Church makes me feel good. It makes me feel like I'm not worthy, sometimes, but that's how we're supposed to feel. Because God tells us we all are sinners. I like to feel like I have a friend in Jesus. He's not just my Savior, but he's also somebody we can go to with our problems. I always feel like I have a personal relationship with him, and it's because of him that I have the success that I have. A lot of people find it hard to pray, I guess. I don't. I worry sometimes that people might think I'm just praying to show people that I'm a believer, but that's not true. It's true in a way, I guess, because I'm certainly not ashamed to be out front about my beliefs. But when I get down on my knees to pray, I'm doing it because I want to thank God or I want to talk with God about something.

"I remember as a kid when Daryle and I slept in the same room, we'd both say our prayers, and he'd finish before I did. He'd ask me what I was doing down there on my knees for so long, but I'd just tell him I had to stay on my knees until I told God everything that was on my mind."

Archie remembers no dramatic turnaround, no overwhelming conversion like Saul of Tarsus had on the road to Damascus.

"I just grew up believing, I guess. My parents taught me the right things, and my mother was always active in church. She was pretty busy with so many kids and she might not have made it to church every Sunday, but God was the center of our home life. I remember the little booklets we had in Sunday school, and I tried to get as much as I could out of them. When I was older, maybe I got to the point where I wanted to make this full-time commitment, but still I didn't think of it as turning my back on a bad life and going into a good one. Maybe it sounds awful, but I really don't remember doing many bad things. I don't think I was a bad boy. So maybe I didn't have that big conversion that lots of people have experienced. It wasn't like suddenly I woke up. It was just that I had a more mature attitude toward Jesus Christ, and I decided I wanted him to be the center of my life.

"Today, lots of people go around saying, 'God, is dead,' and lots of people turn their backs on God. We do have a materialistic world, and there's a lot of sin and prejudice and hatred and all that. But I see lots of young people turning to Jesus Christ, too. The various Christian movements are really growing, and I see more awareness on the high school and college level today. There are more temptations and more trouble for kids to get into, but I feel pretty good about most of the young people I meet. And when people ask me about the way I feel, I try to explain it the best way I can. But I don't have all the answers. Maybe I don't even have a lot of them. But I know what I believe, and I try to tell them my story, and what Jesus Christ means to me.

"I think we have to accept God on his terms and accept things the way he wants them to be. When we pray, I don't think we should expect a drastic change right away. Things will take place in a span of time, when he believes they should take place, not when we want them to, necessarily. When I say a prayer, I don't expect it to happen right then and there. Things might just keep going bad, but eventually they'll work themselves out if we wait upon the Lord. Life has been so good for me, I wonder if maybe there won't come a time when the Lord is going to really test me and put something down hard on me. Christ is with everybody, I know, but I feel he's been really good to me. I just wonder when it's all gonna stop.

"I try to read a lot and find out what God's will is. I read the Bible a lot; I like the modern translations because they're easier to understand. I've read that *Good News for Modern Man,* and every time I pack my gear to go on a football trip, I take something along to read. I can't say that I fully understand the Bible, and I've read it cover to cover several times. But I'm going back through it some more. You know, every time I read it I get more and more out of it. My favorite story is about the prodigal son. It teaches you that no matter what may happen, your parents never forget you, and no matter how bad you may be, they never turn their backs on you."

Loretta and Archie Griffin have already decided on a plan for church attendance when they have children. Loretta gets upset at parents who force church attendance on their children, yet may not attend themselves.

"That seems ridiculous to me for parents to send their children to Sunday school or church, or drive them there and drop them off and not go themselves. It's like saying, 'It's good for you, but it's not necessary for me to go.' Church is good for everybody of all

ages. We believe you have to establish those churchgoing habits
early and stick with them, but more importantly, have the right
kind of Christian home life that makes the children want to become involved, and makes them want to live the right kind of
life."

Archie quickly interjected the scriptural admonition from Prov-
erbs: "Train up a child in the way he should go, and when he is
old he will not depart from it."

Woody Hayes likes to tell how he'd nearly stumble over the
kneeling Archie Griffin each time Ohio State's Buckeyes came
roaring out of the locker room "because Arch'd be down on his
knees praying."

Archie said he never once prayed for victory.

"I always prayed that every man would do his very best. We're
all given certain talents, and Jesus wants us to use them to our
fullest all the time. If you do your best, no one can ask any more.
Then I'd always pray that no one would get hurt. I just never
thought it was fair to pray for victory, and I wouldn't ever pray for
myself to look better than someone else. Just doing my best, that
was enough."

Gus French has seen Ohio State football players come and go,
literally, for years. He's a Columbus policeman whose beat is the
airport.

"I spoke to some of the players the first time they came
through, and Archie was one of them who spoke back," said
French. "Every time after that, he'd make sure to say 'Hello,' and
once in a while if they had a few minutes, he'd stop and chat.
People would flock all around him and he'd always take time, and
the amazing thing is he'd never seem to get rattled. He'd always
have that smile on his face. I've known a few of the so-called
superstars over the years. They all come through here, football
and show business, you name it. But I've never seen one handle
his fame as well as Archie. And he hasn't changed from the first
time he ever got any publicity."

Before Archie Griffin was born, Sam Greenawalt was playing a mighty fine center for Penn football teams, in 1948–49–50. Later, he starred for the Quantico Marines team, coached at Great Lakes, and later was a decorated hero of the Korean conflict. Today, Sam Greenawalt is executive vice president of the Michigan National Bank and not long ago was named recipient of an NCAA Silver Anniversary Award. He got to know Archie Griffin at the NCAA meetings in St. Louis during the basketball season two years ago.

"He's one of those people with a magic about him," said Greenawalt. "There's not an ounce of sham or pretense about him. The more time I spent with him, the more I liked him. If he never carried a football one more time in his whole life, he'd be an overwhelming success. He's bright, he's sensitive, and he's go-oriented. Archie Griffin is one of the truly humble people in this world."

Kaye Kessler is entitled to be considered cynical, since he's been a newspaperman for thirty years and by every measuring stick should be hard and bitter and insensitive after all these years. But an Archie Griffin still makes him melt.

"Sincerity is the key to the whole thing with Archie," Kessler said. "We've been exposed to a lot of great football talent in Columbus, but of all the qualities that go into greatness, Archie has more of them than anyone else."

Kessler covered every Archie Griffin game for four seasons and perhaps has written more words about him than anyone in the world.

"I've never seen him change—not for one minute. He was the same fine young man the day he left school as he was when he arrived. They say success spoils just about everybody, but Archie Griffin has true humility. He's the same with everybody he meets. He's just a nice human being. I've never heard anyone say a bad word about him. You'd have to invent enemies for Archie Griffin."

When Fred Jarvis chronicled Archie's career for the *Journal* of the Downtown Athletic Club in New York for the second Heisman Trophy presentation, he wrote that Archie was on a "non-ego trip."

Jarvis wrote: "One thing we have to be careful of with Archie Griffin: Don't write a eulogy, don't exaggerate, don't get effusive or sentimental. It's just not in character. There's nothing traditionally heroic about griding out one hundred yards every Saturday, nothing that smacks of legend in thigh muscles so bruised and sore every Monday morning that you can barely walk to class —never mind show up for practice. And nothing exciting in merely getting the job done without fuss or histrionics—and that means every job: at home, at school, on the field, in the community. Griffin avoids glamor and publicity and the whole aura of athletic stardom as if it were a vicious secondary, ready to throw him for a permanent loss."

It did not surprise anyone in Ohio that Archie Griffin had that kind of impact in New York. The home folks had known for years that if Archie Griffin had any enemies, they were merely people who hadn't had a chance to know him.

# 4

## *A Different Kind of Game*

Griffin Enterprises was organized in early January 1976, just before the annual draft of football talent by the teams of the National Football League.

Archie would be playing a different kind of game, hopefully for big money. Most of the "money talk" was between older brother Jim and Archie. Decisions that affect any of the Griffins are made by *all* the Griffins, but Jim would be the front man. He'd contact various companies to see if they'd use Archie in advertising and promotion. But every member of the family would share in the profits.

It's not the ordinary way to do things, but it's the Griffin method.

Jim explained: "The family has to know about everything that's happening, but they've entrusted me with the responsibility of making sure everything goes all right in making the various deals. It's my responsibility to report to the others to let everybody know what's going on. But the decisions are pretty much made by Archie and me."

If it appeared extraordinarily greedy of the family to profit by Archie's talent, or extraordinarily naïve of Archie to permit such a situation to develop, that's just a matter of outsiders not understanding how the Griffins operate. Archie said, "It's just the only way to do things. We all believe in it. After all, if it weren't for my parents, I wouldn't have any ability to capitalize on and I wouldn't have had the opportunity to show what I could do."

Prior to the college draft, two of the elder Griffins had more or less established a favorite team in their minds. Papa Griffin leaned toward the Dallas Cowboys "because I think they have a good organization and they'd send Archie some mail every week. I thought they were just more interested in him and they have a pretty good coach in that [Tom] Landry fellow."

Brother Jim liked the Miami Dolphins "because Don Shula likes a good running attack, and besides, the weather in Miami isn't all that terrible."

They had gone down the list of the twenty-six established teams in the National Football League, written down pluses and minuses for each, and tried to analyze where Archie might fit into the draft picture. Things like climate, coaching philosophies, the number of veteran running backs on a particular roster and team strength were all marked down. The Griffins were agreed on one point, and that is that they'd all be terribly disappointed if Archie were not selected in the first round.

And they had heard the familiar criticism about Archie, that he really was too small for professional football, just as he had been too small to play big-time college ball. The others in the family might have been offended by it, but by now Archie had arrived at the point where he could not do without that kind of sniping.

"I really like that kind of challenge. I'm not kidding. I know I just can't ever walk on the field and be a starter. I know it's going to take lots of hard work on my part to prove myself, and that's fine with me. When I got all through at college, I realized I'd have to put all those things I did behind me, and start all over. The big writeups and the awards—you can leave them home when you go to the pros."

It was a cold, raw day in Columbus when the National Football League franchises began the drafting. Archie Griffin had only four teams with more minuses than pluses. They were Tampa Bay and Seattle, the two new expansion clubs, plus New Orleans and San Diego. The Griffin brain trust figured Archie would be the eleventh or twelfth player selected. Archie stayed at his apartment, and some student reporters from the campus newspaper decided to hang around with him. His brother Raymond joined them.

"I had both the television and the radio on, trying to keep up with what was going on. It seemed like I waited forever. When it came time for the Cincinnati Bengals to pick, I thought for sure they'd pick me because we had some inkling they were pretty interested. But they took Billy Brooks, a wide receiver out of Oklahoma, as their No. 1 choice. Down deep, my feelings were hurt. But I didn't realize at the time that the Bengals had two first-round draft choices."

At two other parts of town, Papa Griffin was on the phone with Jim, sharing disappointment that Archie had not yet been tabbed.

Shortly after one o'clock in the afternoon, a secretary from the Cincinnati team called Archie and told him he'd been picked by the Bengals. He, too, was a first-round pick, since the Bengals had two choices in the first round. Archie Griffin was the twenty-fourth player selected by the NFL.

"Sure, I'd like to have been the very first player picked in the whole country. It would have been a great honor, but I really couldn't expect that, and I didn't expect it. Anyway, if that had been the case, I'd have wound up with either Tampa Bay or Seattle, and I'd have gotten creamed."

And so it was, on April 12, 1976, that Archie Griffin became a professional football player. Technically, he was still an amateur because he had not signed a contract, but "in my own mind, that was the day I thought of myself as a professional. And it felt good."

There were lots of volunteers ready to help Archie negotiate his contract with either the Cincinnati Bengals of the NFL or the Montreal Alouettes of the Canadian Football League. Mike Trope, the man who served as adviser to Johnny Rodgers, Anthony Davis, Chuck Muncie, and Joe Washington, was consulted. So was Eddie Elias, who runs the pro bowlers' tour and who has excellent contacts all around the country. But Archie and his older brother had agreed, while Archie was still in college, that it would be Jim Griffin who'd serve as agent. The others would be paid finders' fees, based on deals they might arrange.

The offer from the Canadian interests came quickly. The Alouettes offered a three-year deal worth $290,000, and it included a signing bonus of $150,000. A clause in the contract stipulated that the club could not cut Griffin for three seasons.

"I'll admit that I never really had any interest at all in playing in Canada. But if we could use that offer as leverage with the Bengals, we figured it'd be nice. And if the Bengals didn't offer much at all, we could always take the Canadian deal. We had done a little bit of research on the Cincinnati Bengals and their financial policies, and they have a history of being—well, let's just say they don't throw their money around carelessly."

The Griffins, and Mike Trope, had done other homework, too. They knew that the Bengals, while second in team passing in the American Football Conference in 1975, had only the twelfth-best rushing offense in their conference. Only one team, the San Diego Chargers, had a less productive ground game. And while Ken Anderson again ranked as the top passer in the entire league, there were twenty-eight runners who had more output on the ground than Cincinnati's leading rusher, Boobie Clark. The Griffins knew the Bengals needed help in the backfield.

Meanwhile, the pro football scouts saw five runners they figured had more potential for the rough pro game than did Archie Griffin. Chuck Muncie of California was the third player selected, and he had been drafted by the New Orleans Saints. San Diego followed the Saints by immediately tabbing Joe Washington of Oklahoma in the first round. Purdue's Mike Pruitt went to Cleveland in the first round and was the seventh player selected overall. The ninth player drafted was still another running back, Texas A&M's Bubba Bean, who went to the Atlanta Falcons.

The Detroit Lions had a pair of first-round draft choices and one of them picked Lawrence Gaines, the big fullback out of Wyoming. He was the sixteenth player selected.

Archie, the twenty-fourth collegian selected and the sixth running back, piled into the back seat of his new automobile and let brother Jim and Mike Trope occupy the front seat for the drive to Cincinnati on May 4.

"I didn't want to drive. I was pretty nervous. There was some talk on the way down about how much Cincinnati might offer, but Jim and Mike did most of the talking. I mostly listened."

They left Columbus at 10:30 A.M. and drove directly to the Bengals' office, arriving at noon. They had figured the first offer from Assistant General Manager Mike Brown would be $171,000 spread over three years. And if the Bengals came in very low?

"We were gonna come in very high with a counterproposal and just go from there. We figured one ridiculous offer deserved another ridiculous offer. If they came in really low, we planned to tell them to just match the Chuck Muncie deal in New Orleans: $1.1 million over seven years, with the first five years guaranteed.

"I was pretty nervous when we got to the office, but I didn't want anyone to know it. I knew I wouldn't say a whole lot. We all sat there on the negotiations, and you could feel the tension. The first offer Mr. Brown came up with was pretty good, I thought. He offered me a bonus of $70,000 for signing, then a three-year contract. My salary was to start at $46,000, then go to $52,000 the second season and $60,000 the third season. But only the bonus was guaranteed. It wasn't a no-cut contract. I had to make the team. I thought that was all right. I didn't expect a no-cut deal."

The Griffin camp asked for a time-out and huddled privately for a few minutes before rejoining Mike Brown.

The Griffins proposed a deal halfway between what the Bengals had offered and what Chuck Muncie had received. The Bengals sat on their first offer. Everyone thought it was a good time for lunch.

"I was nervous, but I was hungry, too. I ordered that funny sandwich with the sauerkraut on it."

An agreement finally was worked out at about six o'clock that same evening. The contract includes a nondisclosure clause, and that means the Griffins could not tell anyone the details of the pact. Making public the money figures would mean a loss of his signing bonus.

"It's a good deal, I think. When we shook hands, I didn't feel I had been taken, and I didn't feel I had gotten anything I didn't deserve. I didn't want to have any big arguments or any trouble over the signing. That's no way to start out your pro football career. I just wanted to get it over with and start playing football. I have no regrets about signing."

With the contract negotiations out of the way, Archie and his bride, Loretta Laffitte, enjoyed a brief honeymoon before he headed for Chicago to take part in the annual College All-Star game. It was a rude welcome into the pro ranks the Pittsburgh Steelers provided for Archie and the rest of the All-Star players. The All-Stars showed no offense at all, and the rains came down in such torrents the game had to be suspended. An electrical storm made it impossible to complete the contest—but it wasn't really a contest, anyway.

"I carried the ball two or three times and just couldn't get it going. We ran the Notre Dame offense, I guess, because Mr. [Ara] Parseghian was coaching us. It was a little confusing at first, but only because of the different terminology. We made mistakes, all of us. I made mistakes, and some guys on the line were confused. But the Steelers weren't confused at all. They had great pursuit. They were on the ball almost as fast as we were.

"I'll tell you, I came there expecting the Steelers to be terrific, and they didn't disappoint me. It wasn't a matter of doubting my ability, though. It was a terrible night and the conditions were impossible and the field was too slippery to do anything. I'm not alibiing, but you could tell right from the start it would be a tough night. The first time I carried the ball, L. C. Greenwood caught me in the backfield before I could get back to the line of scrimmage. I mean, he caught me first. Then there were lots of other guys who hit me."

And did the bad, bruising Steelers say anything to the two-time Heisman Trophy winner?

"L.C. did, but I don't know if I should repeat it. I guess it isn't so bad, though. He said, 'Quit running that bullshit.' But I didn't say anything back to him. I just laughed to myself a little bit when I was going back to our huddle. It was kinda funny. It must've seemed like that to him, because I didn't show him much, that's for sure. But they weren't bad guys or anything. As a matter of fact, they were like real friendly on the field. Of course, they could afford to be, couldn't they?"

Archie bolted out of Chicago the morning after the game and headed for the Cincinnati Bengals' training camp at Wilmington, Ohio. Wilmington is a sleepy college town not far from Dayton, and it's nestled snugly in the gentle rolling farm country of southwestern Ohio. It is the custom of NFL teams to conduct training camps in what general managers call "low profile" towns. They try to avoid cities. They'd like their athletes to avoid bars and go-go joints, and most teams are very successful in securing training sites where the athletes almost have to go out and conduct a scavenger hunt to find trouble.

The Bengals would have no such worries with Archie.

The groupies and the camp followers would have no easy time finding Wilmington, anyway, and if they tried they might get discouraged before they arrived in the town, where the streets are clean and where everybody seems to mow his lawn regularly.

Coming from Dayton you pass the Crowbrier Camp Ground. Near the hamlet of Corwin you see two men putting orange paint on a bridge that used to be silver, or putting silver paint on a bridge that used to be orange. Another sign said "Firewood-cutting Permits," but just down the road some bulldozers and other heavy equipment were tearing up a beautiful hillside, building a new road just outside Harveysburg and sacrificing more landscape in the name of progress.

Someone who had flunked spelling had put up a sign pointing

the way to the "Pentecoastal Camp Grounds." There were a number of stands on Ohio Route 73 where a motorist could buy fresh garden produce. Past more well-cultivated fields and neat farmhouses and freshly painted white fences you see the road leading to the Jonah Run Baptist Church, and someone else has put up a sign offering free kittens. It seems there are more American flags on display around Wilmington than in many other sectors of the country. There isn't a single crooked mailbox. All are erect and neatly painted.

Enter Wilmington and you are greeted by a corporation sign reading "This Is a Bicentennial Community." And would it be unpatriotic to yen for a sign, at the entrance to any town in 1976, that said, "This Is Not a Bicentennial Community."

Wilmington is the kind of town where people sit in rocking chairs on their front porches, and on an August day many were doing just that.

This was a different sort of August for Wilmington, because there would be changes in the Bengals. Not only would Archie Griffin be joining the team, but also Paul Brown—for the first time in the history of the franchise—would not be coaching it.

"Don't tell me you'll miss seeing me on the sidelines," he ordered, good-naturedly, "because I know you just like to see me suffer. Actually, it's not difficult to handle this business of not coaching. It's very pleasant, the way it's working out. I've prepared for this mentally."

For all the seasons that Paul Brown has coached, from Massillon High School to Ohio State to Great Lakes to the Cleveland Browns and then finishing up with his own Cincinnati Bengals, there has been the "Paul Brown player."

And already, it was being said that Archie Griffin was drafted because he fit the Brown mold.

"I don't know if there's a Paul Brown type, but I know there is a type of individual we always strive to obtain. We look for people with ability *and* character. We don't want the so-called problem children. We don't want the type of individual who thinks only of himself. You've got to think about the team. You've got to always put the good of the team ahead of the good of the individual. If you find yourself with somebody who can't do that, well, he'll be happy when things are going well for him, and it won't much matter about the team. People of great character always are unselfish, and they'll come through for you in stress situations."

A rap against Paul Brown is that he ofttimes has dealt away or simply gotten rid of good athletes who didn't fit into the Brown mold.

"That's beside the point. You have to do what you believe in your heart is right. Sure, we've had some good physical athletes, and it created some problems when we had to get rid of them. I know I've gotten rid of some talented people. Even during my first season of coaching at Ohio State I got rid of a good player or two, simply because they wouldn't stick to the rules. One fellow went out night-clubbing the night before a game, and we just don't tolerate that sort of thing. So, for the future of our football and what-not, he was dismissed. And we went right along. So if that makes me a cold, hard person, I guess that's what I am. But you have to think of your overall program. You have to think of what is good for the team. You have to think of the future. Lots of people are blessed with ability—but when you get ability and character, like Archie Griffin has—then you have a winner."

The Bengals had scouted Archie through much of his college career, and Brown said his long-time pal Paul Hornung of the Columbus *Dispatch* had been "so high on Archie as a person." The Browns watched Archie perform, then checked his speed and clocked him at 4.5 seconds in the 40-yard dash.

"That's pretty good speed, and some people had questioned his speed. Then we threw him the ball, and he proved he could catch it. The fact that he wasn't as big as some others just didn't matter. He's just an unusual person, and the more we've gotten to know him the more we think of him. He has that great ability to get along with people. He's so honest and forthright and open in everything he does and says—well, he just has an abundance of character. And to get a person of that caliber is really a plus in our business. I believe that every time you take a No. 1 draft choice and you are worried about his character, and you say to yourself that he has all the right numbers for speed and size and agility, and then you say to yourself that maybe he'll grow as a person and become a better human being—well, I just think it's better to take somebody that really fits the mold."

Whatever tab you want to put on it, Paul Brown was talking the "Paul Brown mold."

Surely it must give Brown a great deal of satisfaction that he took a brand-new team, an expansion franchise, and made it a winner more quickly than anyone else in the history of the game. And it is true that the big winners in professional football over the years have been coached, for the most part, by strong disciplinarians like Brown and Lombardi and Shula and Landry and Grant.

"All I know is that I believe in my own system of evaluating talent and evaluating people," Brown said. "You have to go with the quality people and gradually cull out the others. I know one thing: You can't build a good football organization and have a true winner without the main people having character and being the right kind of people. I'll tell you, you never lick what we call the eternal verities. You just can't whip it or get around it. That's the way it always ends up."

Does Brown predict stardom in the NFL for Archie Griffin because of this combination of talent and character?

"I really don't know. Stardom is so unusual, almost rare. It's having so much ability that the pros just can't contain you. O. J. Simpson has that, but very few do. Archie is already a focal point, and I can safely predict that whatever comes his way, good or not so good, he'll handle it very well. He'll wear it well. He'll carry his share, and how much notoriety that commands remains to be seen. He's just magnificent the way he handles people and the adulation that comes his way. He's truly a very humble man."

That Griffin was needed by the Bengals could be seen in the statistics of the previous season. Not a single Bengal runner had gone as much as thirty yards on a single run. They simply had no long-ball threat. Boobie Clark had an off year, with less than six hundred yards gained. Rookie Stan Fritts could smell the goal line and had rushed for eight touchdowns, but he was not much of a threat for the long gainer. Lenvil Elliott had established himself as pretty much of a journeyman performer. Essex Johnson would be traded, after an off year.

Archie Griffin got no message, though, that he would be a starter for the Bengals.

"I looked around and I saw a lot of talent," he said, "so I didn't get any feeling that I had it made. Besides, they had drafted some other running backs besides me [Tony Davis of Nebraska and Randy Walker of Miami of Ohio], and they had Charlie Davis out of Colorado, who missed his rookie year with an operation, and he was coming back. And right away I heard they were thinking of trying Willie Shelby as a runner instead of using him as a spot player."

So the two-time Heisman Trophy winner came to pro camp off a lackluster performance in his first encounter with the big guys, and with a great deal of apprehension and uncertainty.

"They were in a scrimmage game when I got there, so I just went to the sidelines and sort of hung around. Some of the guys kidded me about the game in Chicago."

Jack Donaldson, the offensive backfield coach, talked with Archie a bit and instructed him to be ready to practice on Monday. But Archie really wanted to get into the scrimmage.

"I stood there on the sidelines and watched them cracking and I got those little butterflies in my stomach. I just wouldn't have minded being in there, because I didn't play that much in the All-Star game, and maybe I wanted to get that one behind me."

On Monday, Archie and some other players from the rookie crew—among them Billy Brooks of Oklahoma and Tony Davis of Nebraska—stayed on the practice field after the others had gone to the showers, and put in some extra work with Coach Donaldson.

Archie was not as concerned about his treatment on the field as off it. The hazing of rookies in the National Football League is a long-established tradition. In days gone by the hazing was done with as much brutality in some cases as occurs in some college fraternities. Veterans used to almost totally ignore rookies. After all, their jobs were the ones the youngsters were seeking. Rookies were made to shine shoes, or stand on the tabletops during mealtime and sing their college fight songs or alma maters. It was not uncommon for a rookie with either a poor singing voice or too little volume in his presentation to be made to do the number twice. They were made to run errands, like going after a dozen pizzas, even after curfew. And rookies who complained about the "humiliation" were given extra assignments, and the following year—if they were still around—they'd be among the leaders in the hazing of the new group.

"I'd heard a lot of stuff like that, but none of that went on here. Coy Bacon started kidding me right away, and for a little while I didn't know if he meant it or not. But he's a terrific guy, and he never made us do anything. But he kept threatening us. He'd say, 'Rook, we're gonna make you sing and dance.' I'll never forget when I came into a meeting with the whole team for the first time, he was in the back of the room and he started yelling, 'Where is that Archie Griffin? Where is he? Where is that dude? Where is Archie Griffin, the Heisman Trophy winner? Boy, you rookies don't know how easy you got it. All the guys are gonna dance and sing for us.'

"I didn't know what was happening. I was really scared. I would have danced, that's for sure. But right away, he started coming up to our room and talking with Brooks and me. He's a lot of fun. All the veterans treated me right, right from the beginning."

Just as the stories about rookie hazing were exaggerated, so were the tales about the ostracizing of rookies and the lack of guidance from the veterans.

"They were super, just super. Two guys I would be competing with for one of the running-back jobs—Lenvil Elliott and Charlie

Davis—they pitched right in and gave me some good tips. And I had been told that with everyone challenging for a position, that nobody would be helping anybody else. It was a kind of gang fight, you know, everybody for himself. So when I first got to camp I was scared to ask questions. But right off, everybody was helping me. So later on, when I wanted to know something, or I wasn't sure about something, I'd ask, and they'd all help me."

The Bengals played their first preseason game against the Packers in Green Bay the night of July 31. Archie Griffin had just five days of work with the Cincinnati offense, but he carried the ball a dozen times against the Packers. The output: forty-nine yards and one touchdown.

"I felt all right. Not tremendous, but all right."

The coach, Bill Johnson, announced the next week that Archie would be in the starting lineup for the second game against the Buffalo Bills. It would be a Saturday night game before the home folks at Riverfront Stadium.

"I felt kinda funny, knowing I would start. Actually, I felt bad for Lenvil Elliott. After all, he's been with the club for a few years. I guess I was more nervous before this game 'cause I knew my folks would be there to see me. I spent most of the day in the toilet. I always get those problems with my insides on game day, but it was worse this time. It was almost like I used to get that problem before we'd play Michigan every year in college. That was the worst."

On his first two plays against Green Bay, Archie had gone off tackle for three yards, then caught a screen pass for nine. His longest gain was a twenty-yard scamper.

Things were much better against Buffalo, despite Archie's concern about how his teammates would feel about him getting a starting opportunity. The game was not five minutes old when he burst off tackle, got to the outside, and cut back for a forty-nine-yard touchdown run.

"Maybe it sounds terrible to say this, but I had been thinking about breaking a long run ever since I joined the club. Some folks might think it was corny, but as soon as I got back to the sidelines I got down on my knees and said a little prayer of thanks. The Lord has been awfully good to me, and I wanted to thank Him for that opportunity to use the ability He gave me."

Archie Griffin had said his thanks to God after his very first pro game, in Green Bay. He did not do it on the field for all to see, but he did it without much sleep.

"I was really uptight before the game. I knew I'd be nervous, but it was worse than I imagined. I didn't start the game, and I was jumpy on the sidelines because I wanted to get in there. At least, when they told me to go in, I didn't forget my helmet, and I didn't fumble the ball the first time I touched it. When our chartered plane finally got back to Cincinnati, I drove to Columbus, where Loretta and I had an apartment. I didn't get home 'til five in the morning, but we got up and went to church. I just thought it was the right thing to do. Besides, I had a whole lot to be thankful for. And if you can't make a little sacrifice for God now and then, what kind of a Christian are you, anyway?"

He learned when he got back to camp on Monday that he'd be starting against Buffalo. Knowing that did nothing toward easing the pregame jitters.

"Playing in Cincinnati, I knew my family would be there. And besides, playing before the home folks, who really are paying my salary, puts a little extra pressure on you. And you know the fans are sitting up there wondering what the new guy is gonna do."

Did he worry about having rabbit ears, and hearing some leather-lunged fan yell out something about the two-time Heisman Trophy winner earning his huge salary?

"Not really. I guess some people yelled things at me at some road games when I was in college, but I always try not to let things like that bother me. I believe you have to concentrate. If you let someone know he's getting under your skin, he'll dig a trench there for you. I really didn't have any trouble getting myself up for the Buffalo game. I know it was just an exhibition game, but it was important to me, and I know it was important to our team, too. You have to develop winning habits, and coaches have always told me you have to make sure you have good effort all the time, whether it's in practice or a scrimmage game or whatever. It's easy to get into a slump, and I've always felt a slump is just as contagious as a winning spirit. I knew the coaches would look at a lot of different backs, but I knew I'd start. I just wanted to make the most of the time I had in the game. I was trying to figure out how to make something work in the small amount of time I was gonna be in. I did a lot of concentrating."

The Packers took the opening kickoff, couldn't gain, and had to punt.

On the Bengals' first play from scrimmage, quarterback Ken Anderson called Archie's number.

"It was a straight handoff, and I tried to go off tackle. I guess I got two or three yards, that's all."

The coaches' charts of the game showed what happened on every play and how each player handled his assignment.

On the second play, Anderson called the fullback's number. Archie's job was to fake a handoff. The backfield coach said he carried out the fake satisfactorily.

The third play called for Griffin to pick up the safetyman.

"But a guy ran in front of me, so I hit the guy who ran in front of me. The coach said it was okay."

The fourth play was a pass to the fullback, with Griffin again faking.

"The coach said I could have faked better. I looked at the films and I didn't fake very well at all."

The fifth play was a halfback draw.

"I saw Buffalo coming on a blitz as soon as I got the ball. I remember I split the two linebackers, and right then I figured it'd be all right. One of the linebackers wore uniform No. 55. I don't remember the other guy's number. I really wasn't looking for numbers. I was looking for room. When I got about four yards past the line of scrimmage I thought maybe I could break it."

The touchdown brought down the house. At first blush, the

Cincinnati fans figured the club's money—whether $250,000 or $500,000—was well spent.

Archie carried only five times that night, winding up with sixty-four yards.

"But I felt kinda silly after I scored the touchdown. I felt great when I crossed the goal line, then two dudes jumped on my back. I knew I didn't have to stay in for the extra-point try because I don't play on that special team. I was running like crazy for our bench and I almost jumped up into the arms of my teammates, you know, like you do in college. Then all of a sudden, I noticed no one was jumping up and down and no one was gonna be there to catch me. So I guess I kinda settled down a little bit. The first guy I saw was our center, Bob Johnson, and he said, 'Good run.' I said, 'The hole was there. The blocking was good.' Guys came over and congratulated me. It was a good feeling. When I got to myself I had to laugh a little bit. All I could think about was running off the field and getting ready to jump on one of the guys like we did in college sometimes. But he went right on by me. Man, I really felt stupid. At Ohio State, we'd be all over each other, grabbing each other and everything.

"One of the things I heard when I was getting ready to come to the pros was that players aren't as enthusiastic and all that. Now, after being around a little bit, I think they're enthusiastic. They just don't carry on like they do in college. They're a little older and a little more reserved, maybe. Guys will come up to you and tell you that you played a good game or something like that. I think the players and fans are into the spirit of the game enough. Everybody wants to win. If they didn't, I guess it wouldn't be any fun for me and I wouldn't want to play."

Head Coach Bill Johnson didn't fall over Archie after the Bills' game.

"He just said, 'Good game,' and that was enough. I didn't expect him to do any flip-flops."

There was one thing, during training camp, that really bothered Archie, and that was the squad cutting.

"Some guys who had played pro ball told me not to get too buddy-buddy with other rookies, because you might develop good friendships and then the guys would be gone. But I guess I'm a naturally friendly person, and I just couldn't stay to myself and not talk. I hung with the rookies, mainly my roommate, Billy Brooks. But you wonder about guys' secret thoughts, you know, what's going through their minds. It's tough to be called in and told you're cut, that you can't make it. Maybe some guys know without being told. It really bothered me when some of the guys got cut.

"A few guys got cut my first week in camp. It takes some getting used to. I got to know one of the rookies, Bradley Robinson, real well. He was a basketball player who came to the Bengals as a free agent. I don't know whether he thought down deep he could make the team or not, but he wasn't around very long. I remember one afternoon I told him I was going to take a nap. He said he was going to lie down, too. But when I woke up, he was gone. Just like that. It has to hurt."

Archie's off-the-field reputation was obviously known to the Bengal players.

"I didn't run around yelling at everybody that I'm a Christian, but I guess they knew. I hope it shows, anyway. When I first got to camp, one of the first guys who came up and introduced himself to me was linebacker Ron Pritchard. He's a super Christian, and he told me that he had invited Jesus Christ into his life. We had a good talk."

The chapel services the Bengals held each week before the pregame brunch were well attended.

"We had a full house most of the time, and I know Chris Devlin and Ken Riley and Bo Harris and Pritchard and I talked a lot about our commitments to Jesus Christ. I don't go around grabbing people and asking them, 'Are you right with God?,' but I know we had a certain number of guys who were really hard-core believers and let others know about it. Maybe some other players believed in other ways, or maybe they just didn't want to be as out front about it. All I know is that it gave me a good feeling to see so many guys at the chapel services."

Archie was never asked to give his testimony.

"I would have, gladly, but we always had outside speakers. Maybe it's more effective that way, hearing from someone outside the ball club. We had some dynamic talkers, and I think the team benefited. I know I did."

For some players in the NFL, the chapel service is as close as they get to any kind of a church service. For Archie Griffin, it was an adequate substitute.

"Most of our games are on Sundays and the team is always together and there's just no way you can run out, go to church, and get back. I guess some of the Catholic guys might be able to go to a Saturday evening Mass, but for the Protestants it was chapel or nothing. I really missed not being in church every Sunday, but the chapel service made you feel closer to God."

Archie Griffin's first job in the Bengals' training camp was one of survival. It is a Cincinnati Club policy not to write no-cut contracts, so no matter how much money a player is paid, he still has to prove he can make the club, even if he happens to be the world's only two-time Heisman Trophy winner.

"I'm not gonna say I worried about it, but I was concerned. I knew it wouldn't be easy."

It was more difficult than Archie thought. After 4 preseason games he had gained 197 yards in 38 carries—an average of 5.1 yards per carry. He had scored 2 touchdowns. Then came a pair of injuries that hobbled him for weeks. He suffered a pulled hamstring muscle, than a pulled groin muscle. The rookie, who had never missed a game in 4 varsity seasons at Ohio State, sat out the next 2 games, and things weren't very impressive in his first 2 regular-season games. He gained but 38 yards against Denver and only 15 in 7 carries against the Baltimore Colts. Even a 75-yard showing in the third game, against Green Bay—and his first NFL touchdown in a regular-season game—didn't satisfy Archie.

"It was all right, but I couldn't seem to break free. I don't know what my longest gain was, but it wasn't much [it was for eleven yards], and I wasn't really breaking any tackles. The best thing about that game was that I got to carry the ball a lot, and it helped my confidence when they used me as much as they did."

Archie carried the ball twenty times against the Packers, and besides that, caught two passes. He didn't consider it a lot of work; this is the young man who twenty-eight times during his college career had carried the ball at least that many times.

When the season was over, the Bengals had won ten and lost four, but their playoff hopes had been dashed in a blinding snowstorm November 28 on their own field. They lost to the Pittsburgh Steelers, 7–3, after leading in the game. Playing conditions in the second half were horrendous. But then, both teams had to contend with the weather, and the Steelers won the game and went on to make the postseason playoffs. Their 10–4 record was no better than the Bengals, but they had beaten Cincinnati twice during the regular season, and on that basis, the two-time defending Super Bowl champions got into the postseason action while Archie Griffin and the rest of the Bengals watched.

In the critical game against the Steelers' fabled "Steel Curtain" defense, Archie carried the ball eight times, gained twenty-nine yards, and caught two passes for another dozen yards.

"I've never tried to complain to an official about anything all the time I've been playing football, but I really did catch that last pass. I don't think the official really saw it. I think his vision was obstructed, and he waved it off, saying it was incomplete. But I really caught it, and if they'd have allowed that completion I think we'd have gone in and scored."

The Bengals, after relinquishing their half-time lead of 3–0, showed practically no offense for most of the second half. Finally Cincinnati put together a drive, but the clock was moving inside the two-minute mark. The Bengals were out of time-outs. A completion on the critical pass to Griffin would have given the Bengals a first down inside the Steeler fifteen-yard-line, and perhaps the impetus for the winning touchdown.

"Maybe it was my fault he ruled the way he did. The ball was batted around, and I grabbed it before it hit the ground. Looking back, I should have gotten up and run with it, or made some big show about catching the ball. Maybe I should have jumped up and down. But when I looked up, he was signaling an incompletion. I couldn't believe it. I just said to him, 'I caught that ball. I really caught that ball.' But I knew that wasn't gonna change anything."

Even after that defeat, the Bengals still could have made the playoffs, but they needed a minor miracle. They needed to beat the Raiders in Oakland, which they didn't, and they needed the Oilers to beat the Steelers, and they didn't.

But the Pittsburgh game isn't the one Archie remembers most about his rookie season. The things that stick out most in his mind are negative things, unusual for someone of Archie's bubbly attitude.

"I fumbled twice this year, and that really bothers me. I fumbled in our second game against Cleveland. Two guys hit me, and someone grabbed the ball inside our own five-yard line. I hated that because it really put the pressure on our defensive guys. They just got a field goal and we went on to win the game, though. Then I fumbled on a sweep in the Kansas City game, and one of our guys recovered."

"Lots of guys think fumbling is a physical thing, and I guess sometimes you just can't help fumbling. People knock the ball out of your hands with a punch or something, and they're always grabbing at it. But I think fumbling is sometimes caused by just plain lack of concentration. I've heard people talk about some ball carriers and they say, 'He's just a fumbler, that's all,' and I've even heard some runners talk about their own fumbling and they think they can't do anything about it. But I think they could if they'd just concentrate."

Another thing, you'll never see any of that hot-dog behavior out of Archie Griffin.

"When I first started playing at Ohio State I guess I developed the habit of raising the football in the air when I'd score a touch-down, but I don't make any big show out of it. I just hold it up, then drop it, or give it to the official. I've never spiked the ball or thrown it into the stands or anything like that. I don't think it looks good, and besides, it doesn't prove anything to anybody. And this business of carrying the ball way out from your body like a loaf of bread, that's not for me, either. I'm always thinking 'fumble,' and I try to make sure I keep the football."

Archie tries not to think of the two Houston games at all. He called the first game "my most embarrassing moment in all the time I've played football."

The first game was an unspectacular running performance, twenty-one yards in ten carries and one pass reception for seven yards.

Ever since he came into the National Football League a few seasons ago, linebacker Robert Brazile of the Oilers has been mak-ing life difficult for the opposition.

"I could have taken it if he made it just difficult for me, but he made it impossible. He was blitzing, and it was my responsibility to pick up the blitz. I saw him coming, and I hit him. I thought I struck him pretty good. I put my body right in his numbers, and man, he just ran right over me and sacked the quarterback. He must have knocked me back five yards. I've been hit hard lots of times, but I'd never been bounced around like that. When I got back to the huddle, our quarterback, Ken Anderson, said, 'That's your pickup.' He wasn't telling me anything I didn't know.

"On the very next play, I looked up and here came big bad No. 52 again. He faked like he was going to the inside, so I went in-side after him. But he bounced right back outside and got Kenny again. I was just too embarrassed. I didn't know what to say. And the game was on national television, too. I could just imagine what all those folks back home were saying. And I thought I had some good shots on him, too, but he's big and strong and he put me right on my backside. He talked to me a little bit. He called me a 'little bitty so-and-so,' and once when he came at me he screamed that he was gonna kill me, but I laughed. I figured he was just playing around. He tapped me on my head."

When the two teams played the second time three weeks later, Brazile did not get to the Cincinnati quarterback, but the thought of him doing it bothered Archie Griffin all week during the preparation for that game.

"Man, I couldn't think of anything else but him coming at me. I don't think he got to the quarterback that day, but I had a time with him. When I'd get a pretty good block on him, he'd pat me and say 'Nice play' or something like that. But blocking was the only thing I did that day."

Griffin carried the ball only three times that afternoon and wound up with a net loss of one yard. It was the first time in his career that he had a minus-yardage performance.

The following week he had his first 100-yard-plus achievement as a professional, gaining 139 yards in 13 rushes against the Kansas City Chiefs. His 77-yard touchdown run was the longest of the entire NFL season, for all backs.

Archie remembers Jack Lambert, too, describing the Steelers' linebacker as "the meanest-looking man I ever saw."

"I'd sit up there in the I formation and he'd stare right at me. It seemed like he was trying to stare a hole right through me. He'd be jumping up and down, and he has those front teeth out, and he's always got blood on him. He really looks mean. He could scare some people."

Even Archie Griffin?

"I'm not scared of anybody, but I'll tell you what, I didn't wanna run toward him. If the play called for it, I would, but I'd rather run away from him. I knew Jack before because he played with my brother at Kent State, but on that football field he's one tough guy. He makes you believe he really wants a piece of you, and a whole lot of times he gets it, too."

Archie's pregame nervousness didn't change just because he was getting paid for performing.

"It was just like in college. I never can get a good night's sleep the night before a game. And from the night before a game until we go out on the field, I spend most of my time in the bathroom. My stomach just goes crazy. I don't know what it is, but nothing seems to help. Once the game starts, I'm all right."

Archie accepts that as a sign of concern over doing well, not fear.

"I can't really say I've been afraid of anything or anybody in football. I've been hit hard all my life, but I like to think I've done some hitting myself. But I'm always nervous before games. It's more than butterflies; I really get upset. And it's pretty much the same way before I get up to talk before an audience. It's just that I'm so concerned about not doing well. I want to say and do the right thing."

There are critics who say it is difficult, if not impossible, to equate the violence of football with Christianity. For Archie, it presents no problem.

"The Lord gave me certain talents, and I believe he expects me always to do the best I can when I'm on the field. Football is a game. I get paid for it now, but it's still a game more than anything else. I don't think Jesus wants me to be a sissy out there. He sure wasn't a sissy. There's no way he could have done the things he did if he had been a sissy. The Jesus Christ I know is a strong person, a tough guy. And he took a few cheap shots in his time and he had to overcome a lot of obstacles and he told his followers they'd have to endure a lot to make it.

"That's the way I feel. I read the Bible and it doesn't tell us it's gonna be easy. As a matter of fact, it says lots of places that the Christian will have it tougher than the nonbeliever. I've taken some cheap shots in football, but I don't think I've ever given out any. I wouldn't want anyone to do it to me, so I don't do it. I've had a lot of late hits, but I try not to think about them. I try not to question a man's motives for doing something like that. Maybe a guy's got his momentum going and he can't stop. I don't know. I just try to stay cool and try to keep from losing my temper. I remember twice in my rookie pro season they called late hits, once against some guy from Cleveland and another time against a guy with the Jets. But I'm not saying they were deliberately trying to hurt me. I just consider things like that some of the obstacles in my way."

At the same time, Archie Griffin does not deny that football is a sometimes violent game, and he's concerned about the very future of sports.

"You take a look at the whole picture and you have to be concerned. Guys are making fabulous amounts of money and some teams are in big trouble financially and some leagues have folded. Sure, you worry about that and you wonder where it all will wind up. I don't have the answer, but I know some players are really worried about it. Another thing that's getting to be a problem is the behavior of the fans. I didn't see any trouble in Cincinnati, but I know in some pro towns it can get pretty bad with fans throwing things out of the stands at the players.

"I got heckled in Green Bay in my first pro game, and it kinda bothered me. I had been with the team only a few days, and I didn't get into the game until the third quarter. While I was standing on the sidelines lots of people in Green Bay started yelling at me and talking about the Heisman Trophy and asking me why I wasn't playing. After a while, though, I just laughed it off.

"I remember when I was in college, I got hit in the face a couple of times by some fans throwing snowballs out in Iowa, and up in Wisconsin some people were throwing beer cans at our players. Things have gotten pretty violent sometimes in hockey and football and even basketball, and people say it's just a sign of the times. I don't know what it is, but I think we better do something to turn it around."

Whenever Archie Griffin has to field a tough, sometimes loaded question, he responds with candor. But will stop short of condemnation of another human being. He'd prefer to think that perhaps the idiots who threw the snowballs in Iowa or the beer cans in Wisconsin or the fans who pelt pro players with an as-

sortment of objects ranging from bolts to golf balls need a little
guidance, a bit of direction in their lives. Maybe their lives have
not been easy, so let's try to understand their frustration rather
than answer their violence with more violence.

As for today's athlete, who sometimes appears to have "today"
as his god and who may ignore a youngster begging for an autograph and who may not understand that he owes more to the
public than a decent performance, Archie feels nothing but com-
passion:

"It all goes back to the home. Maybe a guy grew up in an atmosphere where that kind of thing wasn't taught. Maybe the
guy who's a bigot grew up with bigotry. Maybe he was taught to
be prejudiced. Maybe it was drummed into him that he's better than someone else. Sure, I wish everyone would take a look
at the times we live in and the social conditions we have in this
country, and I wish everyone would have a little more charity
and love for fellow human beings. I've seen so much need, everywhere I've been. I'm not saying I'm better because I try to give
some of my time to folks less fortunate, and I don't go around
saying it's gonna get me any closer to Heaven. It's just what I
believe. It's just the way I wanna live my life. Sure, I hope some
kids turn out better because maybe Archie Griffin has tried to
be a good example for them. We all sow some seeds of one kind
or another.

"Sometimes I'm tired and I've been on the go but I still have
trouble saying 'No' when I see someone less fortunate and they
need my help. Let's face it, the Bible tells about the parable of
the talents, and I think Archie Griffin has been given a whole lot
more in certain ways than a lot of people. Everywhere I go I see
people of all ages that I know didn't have the kind of home life I
had. So I gotta figure they didn't have as good a start in life as my
parents gave me. Those are the ones I have to share with. But you
know, if you go around trying to get credit for it, then that makes
it all wrong, too. But I'd be lying if I said I didn't get something
out of it. It makes me feel better, and that's a good enough reason

for doing it. Every time I experience something like that, I pray about it, and I pray two ways: I pray for the person who isn't as well off as I am, and I give thanks for what I've been given."

Archie Griffin searches Scripture for direction on how best to witness for Jesus Christ. He says he wants to be a strong witness, "but I don't want to turn people off by trying to force my beliefs down their throats.

"It's tough to know just what to do. Every chance I get I tell people I'm a Christian. I tell people I voted for Jimmy Carter not just because of what I believe he'll do for underprivileged people, but because the man's a Christian. I was really happy when he came out with that because, you know, we're told to do that. We need more people who'll witness and more people who have character. People with real character, I mean a genuine moral commitment, can change the shape of the whole world. If we have enough people with a high moral standard and a sense of duty about what's right, why, the whole course of history can be changed. Not overnight, but it can be changed."

The twenty-eight teams in the National Football League spend millions of dollars each year scouting college talent. Not just the seniors are scouted. They're scouted more seriously, but it is not uncommon for professional scouts to begin keeping tabs on an outstanding prospect beginning with his sophomore season.

The press guide may list a tackle as a hulk of a man, 6-feet-5 and 275 pounds, but when scouts get serious about a prospect they bring their own yardsticks and scales. The program notes may tell you a back runs the 40-yard dash in 4.6 seconds, but the NFL talent scouts bring their stopwatches just in case.

The Dallas Cowboys have the most sophisticated scouting and personnel appraisal system in the league. Theirs is computerized, and measures a flock of skills and aptitudes. But even the Cowboys cannot measure heart and desire. Crusty old scouts like to point to their chests and bellies and say "You just never know what's inside a young man."

Simply put, they're saying that it's not possible to tell how much heart, fortitude, grit, and gut a man has for the rugged game of professional football.

Just like some universities gain reputations as havens for freaks and troublemakers, some professional football teams have become known as sanctuaries for offbeat characters.

Former All-Pro linebacker Joe Schmidt, who had several frustrating seasons as coach of the Detroit Lions before hurrying back to his lucrative businesses, believes the professional football teams could do better scouting jobs with a little more investigative work and less sophistication.

"You simply have to have people with character in order to win," he said. "The draft is supposed to balance out the talent, and I think to some degree it has been successful in doing that. But so many teams make mistakes in judging the character of a young man. I've never understood why there's not more checking into the man's background. What kind of family life did he have? What kind of environment did he live in? What was he like in school? Was he good about attending classes? Did he get along with his friends and teammates? Was he a leader, or someone easily swayed? Did he get good grades? Is he a quick learner? How did he get along with his coaches? Did he take direction and coaching well? Did he listen? Is he a disciplined individual, or just an individualist? I'm telling you, I played with some great people and with some not-so-great ones. And I coached some outstanding people and I had some rinky-dinks who were impossible to coach. It may sound corny, but winning teams generally have great character. Forget that old line about building character during losing seasons. You either have character or you don't. If you do, you'll wind up ahead of the guy who doesn't have it."

Joe Schmidt was a Paul Brown-type player. When he coached the Detroit Lions, however, he was saddled with too few Paul Brown-type performers.

Bill Johnson is cut from the same bolt of cloth. An outstanding college performer at Texas A&M, he became an All-Pro center with the San Francisco 49ers and then stayed on with the club as an assistant coach for a dozen years before grabbing an opportunity to join Brown with the Cincinnati Bengals. He served as Brown's right-hand man for eight seasons before Brown tabbed him for the main job.

No one should have been surprised. Johnson, too, is a Brown type.

The decision to make Archie Griffin a No. 1 draft choice was not something forced upon a new coach.

"There was no question about his ability," said Johnson. "But there was another dimension to the young man that we absolutely loved. With Archie, you really could measure those intangibles like desire and determination and his love for the game. It oozed out all around him."

Johnson recalled going to the Ohio State spring practice sessions ahead of Archie's senior year. Coach Hayes keeps a chart prominently displayed on the wall, and it shows the number of practice sessions a player has attended. A player might miss practice for a variety of reasons—a classroom conflict, an injury, or sheer laziness.

"Here was the Heisman Trophy winner and a guy who got banged around in every game he played, and he never missed a single practice. That showed me something right there. It showed me he wanted to play. Lots of people have ability, but often something sidetracks them and takes away some of that talent. But when you combine talent and love of the game, you really have something."

Johnson and Archie didn't meet again until the evening Archie had been drafted.

"I remember his coming into the office at Cincinnati and he was just bubbling. I know he wanted to play in Cincinnati because it's close to home and all that, but I'm convinced he'd have felt good no matter what team had selected him. He simply exudes happiness, and it spills out on everyone who comes into contact with him. I was really impressed with him. He's been magnificent right from the start."

When Archie joined the Bengals, the coach made it plain the rookie would not be a "workhorse" runner, as he had been throughout his college career. At Ohio State, Archie averaged twenty carries per game.

"You just can't do that in this league," Johnson said, and he explained it just that way to Griffin. "Our game isn't structured that way, and besides, that's far too much pounding for one man. I know Archie was accustomed to that, and he loves to play so much that he'd carry the ball on every play if we asked him to."

If Archie was concerned he wouldn't play enough, there were some Ohio State fans who feared he'd be used too much. Some of them wrote letters to Johnson, urging him to treat Archie with special handling and not overuse him.

"First, it takes time to get into the pro system. It's a brand-new game. Football is basic blocking and tackling and execution and all that, but the pro game is different in so many ways. People are so much stronger and faster. Perhaps the most difficult adjustment a player coming out of college has to make is the realization that *everyone* in the pros is talented. Everyone has ability. Everyone is an exceptional player.

"For a back, he has to learn quickly that the linebackers are really fast and they're gonna catch him. There's great movement in the game. Even some of the big 260-pound linemen have tremendous speed, so it's tough to run away from people. Archie had a seventy-seven-yard run this year against Kansas City, and it turned out to be the longest run from scrimmage of the entire National Football League season. Years ago, there were lots of long runs, but not any longer. The game is too fast. The defenses are too quick, and they just don't let you get loose for the long ones."

The Bengals devised a plan for Archie Griffin's first season in the pros. He'd be broken in gradually, sharing a running back's job with Lenvil Elliott in the early games. It would take some time for Archie to absorb the technical parts of the Cincinnati system, even though the Bengals quickly found him to be a "quick study."

He'd have to learn to run pass routes. At Ohio State, a pass route was akin to a road detour that you took when all other plans went awry.

"That was a big adjustment for him," Johnson said. "But even on the running plays, he wasn't doing quite the job early in the season that he did later on as the year progressed. If you made a graph on Archie Griffin's performance from start to finish this past season, over the twenty games including the preseason games, you'd see that graph gradually going up week by week. He just got better and better. And he'll get a whole lot better now that he's into the system. Next year, we plan to use him a lot more, not just running but also catching the ball. You watch, he'll be an outstanding performer."

Johnson believes Archie could have been a thousand-yard achiever in his rookie season had it not been for an injury that slowed him down at the very beginning of the campaign.

But another factor that weighs heavily on any rookie is the mere fact of being a rookie.

"Let's face it, you're thrown from a college campus into a business. Pro football is a sport, sure, but it's a business. And it's a tough business. You've been on campus where the atmosphere is pretty much a fun thing, and you're with your own age group. Suddenly, you're tossed into a whole new set of circumstances. You have a total environment change. You're in with older men, some of them approaching forty years old. They're professionals, and have been for a long time. They're pretty proficient at what they do. And, to be truthful, they're a pretty protective group. It's a tough thing to say, maybe, but it's a dog-eat-dog business. I never thought of it as a culture shock, but I guess in reality that's what it is.

"Pro football is a rigorous, mental routine. It's a game for really tough people. You're separated from your family, you're in a full-time profession, and the mental discipline required is staggering. We play twenty games, and we have three weeks before that to get ready for the first one. It's a long, tough grind. I really don't believe the average fan comes close to understanding what it takes out of a player to stick it out. We hear a lot of players today talking about quitting after a few years. I'm not surprised. For a man to last ten years in the pro game, that's really something. You hurt a lot in ten seasons. That's why a lot of players just can't take it."

Like every other coach, Bill Johnson has seen players of extraordinary skill simply pack it in. Some of them have left training camp in the dark of the night without even leaving a note. They just could not take the grind and had to escape it.

"In a lot of ways, football hasn't changed a bit since I pulled on my first uniform back in the sixth grade in Tyler, Texas. It still requires toughness and dedication and all that, and the teams that have the most discipline, and block and tackle best, still win. But the game has become much more sophisticated, much more complex, and in many ways the pressures on the people in the game have become intensified. I look at some rookies and I know they're scared. They have every right to be. It can be a scary experience. It's a different world, one of almost total isolation. I've never known a player to last very long in the National Football League without being a real man."

Johnson admitted that in more than twenty years of coaching in the NFL, he's run across a multitude of players who give this dedication and accept this discipline grudgingly because of the rewards involved, "but Archie Griffin does it because of a great love for the game and because it just wouldn't be possible for him to engage in anything without giving his very best."

The captain of the Bengals, center Bob Johnson, had lavish praise for Griffin after his rookie season was over.

"I think a guy in his position comes in with 2½ strikes against him. He was so well known that guys were ready to take a potshot against him, jump on him whenever he made a mistake. But he never said more than a few words, and he always had a smile on his face and words of encouragement for the guys. I don't think anybody who won the Heisman Trophy twice could have come in and gotten accepted as well as Archie did."

Like the Ohio State teammates some seasons before, the Bengals learned quickly that Archie is for real, that Archie really is that good a human being, and that he is, as they say in the business, a straight-arrow kind of man.

Coach Johnson said he liked the idea of the pregame chapel services for two reasons. One, he confessed, is a selfish reason.

"I like anything that brings people together and creates unity, so from a strictly selfish standpoint, I like the idea of the players being together for a common cause. Now, from the religious standpoint, I think it's great, too. I believe people of strong conviction are winners, and I like that.

"After the season was over, I was talking with one of our fine linebackers, Ron Pritchard, and out of a clear blue sky he brought up something about that. Just before we took the field for our first exhibition game, up in Green Bay, I asked Ron to lead our club in a pregame prayer, and he told me he really appreciated that. It really meant something to him. And believe me, it meant something to me when months later he thanked me for it. It shows what kind of a human being he is. He's a man of strong conviction. He also happens to be a terrific football player.

"I'll tell you, it's really refreshing to find people like Pritchard and Griffin. And they're not the only ones; there are lots of them. But in a time in our society when people are voicing their dissent and releasing their frustrations in all sorts of ways, it's meaningful to hook up with human beings like that. You know, we've had players talk over the years about being in a business or sport that dehumanizes them and all sorts of bunk like that. No man can be dehumanized unless he lets it happen to him."

It was often said of Johnson's boss and predecessor, Paul Brown, that he was cold and aloof and maintained a calculated distance between himself and his players. Johnson is a little more outgoing and perhaps maintains a closer relationship with his players.

"I was an assistant coach here for so long that I got to know the players real well, but I can say this: Not from Day 1, when I became head coach, has any player ever tried to take advantage of that. I don't know whether you can say I'm close to the players. I like to think that I'm close to them, but by the very nature of my job there's a natural separation. I know them, and they know me, but there's a clear-cut chasm there. They don't come to me with their problems, yet I'm not what you'd call an aloof guy.

"My thinking about football is very similar to Paul Brown's. My thinking about people is very similar to Paul Brown's. I'm not as disciplined and not as restrained as Paul Brown, but the principles he's built into every team he's been involved with are the principles I'd like to think I can uphold. Principle will win the tough games. There's so much adversity in this business that you have to have principle. You cannot possibly have forty players and all of them with great character, but you have to have an abundance or you're in trouble.

"I've grown up in football. I've been in it all my life. And there are some things that never change. The problems are the same, and the challenges are the same. I don't see a nickel's worth of difference from the time I played football in the sixth grade to now, and that's a span of about forty years. It's a game of skill, but it's a game of emotion, a game of mental discipline and preparedness. All things being even, the team with the mental edge will win. You can take the play books from all the teams in the National Football League, throw 'em out in the middle of the field, stir 'em up, and have everyone grab a different book, and it wouldn't make any difference in the world. There are differences in terminology, and some little twists here and there, but they're minor ones. We all steal from each other anyway. I had a coach not long ago tell me he took every one of our game films and copies down our entire offense just because he liked the way we did it. And so what?"

Once his first season was over, Archie did not ask the Bengal brass how he had done. It would have been totally out of character.

"When I was picking up my stuff after the season, Coach Johnson and Mr. Brown told me I had a real good season. I think it was all right, but I wanted to carry the ball more. But I realize I had so much to learn. I had to do a lot of blocking, and I had to learn all about running pass routes. It's funny, some people saying I was too little and that I wouldn't make it and other people figuring I'd go in and have a super year right away.

"People may not believe me when I tell 'em, but my major concern was making the team. I didn't have any big ideas that I'd be a star or anything like that. After all, I had a lot to learn, and I still do. And when you get into the pros, no one cares how many awards and trophies you've won or how much publicity you've had. You have to prove yourself all over again. For me, my first year was a challenge—to make the team, to get a feeling of belonging. Next year, it'll be another challenge—to play more, to contribute more, to learn more, and to help our team get into the playoffs. I'm sure there'll be a challenge every season I play. When there's no challenge, some of the fun of playing goes out of it."

Of all the honors that have come to Archie Griffin, there is one that is more meaningful than any of the others. He was told, after he won his second Heisman Trophy, that Eastmoor High School had decided to rename its football field after him. The actual dedication came last fall, and Archie came back to Columbus for the occasion.

"I couldn't believe it when they told me they were gonna name it Griffin Field. I found out when I spoke at an awards assembly, and I had nine months to think about it. When the time came, I still was numb. My folks were there, Loretta was with me, and so were Keith and Crystal and Daryle and his wife, Debra. It was raining, but Eastmoor beat Watterson, and nothing could have spoiled that night for the Griffin family. The beautiful thing was that my family was there. They can call it whatever they want, but in my mind I'll always consider the place was named for my whole family. It just has to be that way."

Of the forty-one men who have won the coveted Heisman

Trophy, college football's most prestigious award, perhaps forty of them would trade all their other honors in order to keep the Heisman. Archie Griffin is the only man in history to win two Heismans, and he'd sacrifice both of them rather than erase that name from his old high school field.

For Archie knows that the trophies, like the talent, will fade.

"There are temporary things, and there are lasting things. Every time something good happens to me, I can always find something in the Bible that keeps me in line. Jesus spoke often about being able to handle success. It says in Scripture that it doesn't do us any good if we gain the whole world and lose our own soul. I love the story about the rich young ruler who wanted eternal life, but he didn't want it enough to give up his worldly possessions. Then there's that story about the Pharisee and the publican going into the temple to pray, and you know, the Pharisee was supposed to be so good. He thought he was, anyway, because he gave his money and he spent time in prayer. And he even told God how good he was and that he wasn't like other men. He really thought he was something and that other men weren't as good as he was. And he was wrong, and the Bible tells us that he wound up in trouble.

"But the poor publican was really a humble person. He was so humble in the sight of God that he wouldn't even lift up his eyes. Then in Romans I read a really good passage about how we're supposed to freely give, and the emphasis is on 'freely.' And time after time the Lord has told his people not to exalt themselves. Being grateful for what we have and having a certain amount of pride in what we accomplish is one thing, but we have to be careful not to exalt ourselves. He told his people that if they humble themselves, they'll be exalted.

"I've read the Sermon on the Mount over and over again, and every time it gets more beautiful and more meaningful for me. If you put those words in your heart and use them as a guideline for your life, there can't be any confusion about what God wants us to do and what kind of a person he wants us to be. It's awfully plain. He said we're not supposed to lay up treasures for ourselves here on earth, and Jesus said that if we first seek the kingdom of God and his righteousness, he'll take care of every need we ever have. And I believe that."

*Epilogue*

Not too many years ago, a country singer named Bill Anderson recorded a song, "Where Have All the Heroes Gone?"

The truth is, many of them were gunned down in a society that sometimes seems bent on destroying itself.

Too often, we find that those we hero-worship have feet of clay, too. Like the rest of us, they are overcome by temptation in a hurry-up world that seems largely commercial and hedonistic. There are as many explanations as there are symptoms, and none makes a whole lot of sense. Those who study human behavior tell us we are caught up in a sickness that dictates that we take care of No. 1. It is said that we are a noninvolved society.

People seem pretty content to be spectators, and our cynicism has reached such epidemic proportions that we hoot at Grantland Rice's old line, ". . . and when The One Great Scorer comes to write against your name, He writes not that you won or lost, but how you played the game."

We seem to take for granted such things as hypocrisy in the church, immorality in the home, scandal in public office, thievery in the trade union, chicanery in commerce, and murder in the streets.

Can we then expect our athletes to behave any differently?

Should it surprise us that they have organized themselves into unions? Should we be shocked when the daily sports reports are saturated with stories about athletes being into drugs, playing out options, demanding to be traded, striking, rebelling against coaches and management? Are they not entitled to be as greedy and self-centered as the owners? Can we expect them to exhibit loyalty and dedication and self-sacrifice when they see so little of those things in the so-called outside world? Are these athletes not merely a reflection of the Great American Way of Life, vintage 1970s?

It is written that it is easier for a camel to pass through the eye of a needle than for a rich man to enter into the Kingdom of Heaven. Then is it not more difficult for a star athlete to remain level-headed when all about him he sees nothing but praise on one hand and temptation on the other?

It is uncommon, almost rare, to find an athlete totally unspoiled by this lavish attention.

But such a man is Archie Griffin. He's barely twenty-three years old, but he has wisdom and moral strength well beyond his years. There is not a single chink in his armor. We searched for them, not out of some wild urging to find fault with a larger-than-life creature, but merely as a seeker of truth.

He is a breath of fresh air on a muggy day. He is stability in a world of turmoil. He is concern in a sometimes unfeeling society, kindness in an often selfish world. He's more than a jock. His world is larger than just a football field. He has education, and more than that, he has character. Archie Griffin is a good man—as good as they come.

*Dave Diles*